Also by Dr. Judith Briles

Stabotage!

Money Smarts for Turbulent Times

Zapping Conflict in the Health Care Workplace

The Confidence Factor—Cosmic Gooses Lay Golden Eggs

Money Smarts—Personal Financial Success in 30 Days!

Stop Stabbing Yourself in the Back

Woman to Woman 2000

The Briles Report on Women in Healthcare

10 Smart Money Moves for Women

Smart Money Moves for Kids

Divorce—The Financial Guide for Women

GenderTraps

The Confidence Factor: How Self Esteem Can Change Your Life

When God Says NO

Money Sense

The Money $ense Guidebook

Raising Money-Wise Kids

Woman to Woman

Judith Briles' Money Book

Faith & $avvy Too!

Money Phases

The Woman's Guide to Financial Savvy

The Workplace

Self-Confidence and Peak Performance

Co-Authored Books

Show Me About Book Publishing

The Tango of Authoring and Publishing

The SeXX Factor

The Dollars and Sense of Divorce

The Workplace

Author

YOU

It Takes a Village to Create and Market Your Book

Creating and Building Your Author and Book Platforms

Dr. Judith Briles

The Author **YOU** Series

MileHigh Press

Mile High Press, Ltd.
www.MileHighPress.com
MileHighPress@aol.com
303-627-9179

Books may be purchased in quantity by contacting the publisher directly:
Mile High Press, Ltd., PO Box 460880, Aurora, CO, 80046
or by calling 303-627-9179

Editing: John Maling, EditingByJohn@aol.com
Cover and Interior Design: Nick Zelinger, NZGraphics, NZGraphics@comcast.net
Illustrations: Don Sidle, www.DonSidle.com, DSidle@comcast.net

Briles, Judith,
     Author YOU: Creating and Building Your Author and Book Platforms

ISBN: 978-1-885331-41-0 (hard cover)
ISBN: 978-1-885331-44-1 (e-book)

LCCN: 2012948556

1. Publishing   2. Self-Publishing   3. Author   4. Author Platform

First Edition   Printed in the United States

Dedicated to all my Book Shepherd clients who had the Vision,
Passion and Commitment to create their books and make a difference.

Why the Author YOU Model is the best way to achieve success in publishing today

WOW ... You are thinking of writing a book. So is 80 percent of the population ...

What will separate you from the masses ... those that sell less than 100 books? Do you have the "right stuff" to create a winning book and make a visual presence in today's market? How will you be heard above the author and book noise? Will you be successful?

The "right stuff" is seeded from the get-go by one thing: successful authors think of their authoring and publishing experience as a business. All businesses have models. The *Author YOU Model* is about building the Platforms that create the foundation of your future empire.

Millions of books are published in all formats each year; a great majority should have stayed in the desk drawer. R. Bowker reported that of the approximate 500,000 ISBNs issued in 2011, over 211,000 were issued to what now is identified as the self-published and independent markets. That's a WOW. Almost parity with the "big boys"—the traditional publishers that ruled the publishing channels just a few years ago.

The rest of the published books, those without ISBNs, are in the vanity press, some form of hybrid publisher or in eBook format.

Those are the books that routinely are not edited, have a cut-and-paste quality to the interior and exterior designs ... and are, let's face it, mediocre. Those are the books that you would normally not put on your book shelf to read over as well as admire the look and feel of.

The *Author YOU Model* that is revealed within the pages of this guidebook, the basis of your Platform, has similarities to any business: financial sustainability, marketing strategies, action plans and the ability to fine-tune and reassess as you go along.

As an author, you evolve ... you have to. Publishing is morphing on a daily basis. The savvy author knows it, takes advantage of it and embraces it.

Author YOU.

The *Author YOU Model* reveals the Village that will create the stepping stones to your success. It will deliver the goods to soar you through the author and book noise ... to be heard above the crowd.
It will save you thousands of dollars by keeping you focused and avoiding costly errors. It identifies your options so that you have a better grasp of which road is best for you. And it empowers you to clear the clutter.
Get ready for a visual journey. I've structured many books using Post-its®—different sizes and colors to mark chapters, themes within them, stories and key points. You will find them within *Author YOU: Creating and Developing the Author and Book Platforms*.
Get out your pen ... you've got a series of Activities, all designed to develop the Author YOU in You.

Reading *Author YOU: Creating and Building the Author and Book Platforms* and integrating the *Author YOU Model* will create a *significant advantage* over other authors who use the hit-and-miss method for their book journey.

Most authors write (a good thing); few get their work professionally edited (a bad thing); and fewer still understand the dollars, cents and sense of the publishing game (another bad thing). By using the steps and guides on the roadmap included throughout what's in your hands, you move into the top tier of authors. You gain author power and presence … and success … the success that you seek, as you, and only you define it.

The *Author YOU Model* is all about sustainability. Sustaining you as a person … and creating and sustaining your authoring/book business. Sustainability.

How are you going to create Income—those moneys that will allow you to eat, sleep, play and grow your author/book business?

Platform building is all about foundations and blueprints. Without them, a building crumbles. You are no different. Platform building always starts with a Vision, nourished by and with—Passion; fertilized by your Commitment in the forms of time, energy and money. The People will then come—your customers, book buyers and fans.

You start with Key Questions:
1 What's your Vision?
2 What's your Passion that will—is needed—to support it?
3 How Committed are you?
4 Who are your People—the Customers who will buy your Book?
5 What benefit will you bring to your People?

Book buyers—your People—are looking for one of two things:
- Answers and Solutions
- Entertainment

Which do you deliver … or do you deliver both? If you are a writer of fiction—you easily fall into the entertainment category—sometimes with suspense, shock, weird concepts, belly-laughing humor, anything that your amazing imagination brings forth … a way for your People to drop out and enjoy several hours. If you are a nonfiction author—the answers, solutions and information you provide. You become a master of insight and know-how … you have the magic wand to relieve the pain that your People are facing. It's a good place to be in whether you write fiction or nonfiction.

Part of the **Author YOU Model** is to know clearly who your People are. When you do, your writing Job and your book Connects and delivers the homerun you are looking for.

Every Successful Author has a Model and Platform … what's yours?

Your success is not going to come from the good fairy dropping in and sprinkling dust here and there. Oh, you may feel one or two drop in … but the truth is … your success will come within the Model you create to develop, create, launch and market your book. Oh, and how you bring in sales.

Every … every … successful author needs sales. Writing the book is one thing. Breathing economic life into it is another. Even if you have the means to underwrite it all yourself; you may even say that you don't need any money—you will donate all sales to a favorite charity; you still will have some bills to pay. Think staff, paid-for-hire or outsourcers that will become your marketing arm; think about those who created the book—designers, illustrators, editors and consultants; think about the book manufacturers—the printers physically created it and who put it in your hands; think, think, think. They don't work for free—you need revenue to pay them for what they deliver to you.

Even if your plan was to donate everything and give your books away for free to your People—what happens if your world goes flip-flop? And the People expect the train to keep chugging along? Will you have the means to underwrite it, even in perpetuity? When it comes to creating and building any type of venture … and here, it is you as the author … income is desirable. Income means breathing. Sustainability. Whether it's surplus or break-even revenue, it's the money that enables your Vision to grow. Without it, it doesn't.

Your *Author YOU Model* takes all that into effect. You see, by being successful, your circle expands. Visualize—it's inevitable. The People will and do come. With the help of the Author YOU Model, you clearly define and know what your Mission is—who your People are—what your Book is about.

Sustainability ... *Don't leave your day job without it.*

Terms to Help You As You Enter the Village

People

Your book is for ... *who*? People, but which People? Focus ... the more that you can be specific, the greater your audience can become. When you say anything that looks, sounds or feels like "everyone," you defocus. Not all the people want or need your book. Identify who does.

Significance and Value Provided

What do your People need? Answers? Problems identified? Solutions? Entertainment? What? You and your Book should be significant to them in delivering what they are seeking.

Outlets

Today's reader wants books in a variety of forms. What's yours?

Staying Connected

You initiated communicating with your words ... how are you staying connected? The Internet has a variety of options. What platforms and what else are you using?

Income

Money. Authors want to see cash come in the doors. Where will yours come from? Royalties, special sales, direct sales, up-sales, spinoffs, joint-venture sales, webinars, teleseminars, consulting, speaking ... where?

Key Resources
Books don't happen by themselves. Who's in your village? Printers, designers, illustrators, cartoonists, editors, photographers, researchers, assistants, publishing consultants, coaches, mentors, family, readers, endorsers, publishers ... who else?

Joint Venture Partners
Where Key Resources get the book to the birthing place, Joint Venture Partners (JV) can get it up and running. They have their own People and delight in telling them about you and your book. Who and where are yours?

Outlays
Time, Energy and Money flow ... where will you be spending it; what goods and services do you need; and what time commitment will you personally dedicate? Publishing means getting and staying educated and means moneys will be spent on an ongoing basis. Resources and Joint Venture Partners and their care and feeding are huge. Marketing is critical, and what about You ... what's the cost of your time, energy ... and stress?

Key Activities
Anything that you need to do to create Income, Connection, Outlays, Significance and Value, Marketing, Resources ... anything.

DumpZone
Oh boy ... don't we all think our ideas are fantastic ... and discover that they don't work, they don't fit ... and you seriously wander, "What was I thinking ..." This is the DumpZone, all authors need one to just toss and forget. And as a reminder, don't get detoured again.

Visuals and Activities Say Thousands of Words.

I've written books totally around sticky notes—I routinely use them. Whether they are the official Post-It® or all the knock-offs, it doesn't matter. What I've got in my hands is a palette to start the creation—let the ideas pour forth. Doodles are on some, goofy cartoons pinned or taped on a board to remind me of something (or in some cases keep my spirits up), even a headline or two that catches my fancy. I must admit, my all-time favorite came from one that I spied while waiting at the grocery store. "I gave birth in a snake-infested tree," shouted an interior headline from a *National Enquirer* story. I've never been able to use it until now ... but you never know. It tickled my imagination—I mean, after all, what was she thinking?

Within *Author YOU: Creating and Building the Author and Book Platforms*, you will find plenty of visuals and sticky notes to goose and guide you. Activities are sprinkled throughout—your task is to engage in and complete as you go through. My words and examples will guide you.

Visuals and Activities create your roadmap with exits, detours, warnings and rest stops. And of course, a destination at the end—Your Book.

1

Platform Prepping

2

What's In Your Platform?

3

The Passion Factor

4

The Vision Factor

5

The Commitment Factor

6

The People Factor

7

Keeping Your Platform on the Right Track

8

The Publishing Siren and Your Muse

9

The Time Factor

10

Social Media Creates Your Platform

11

Internet Checklist for People Platform Building

12

The Money Factor

Yours Can Be in the Bank, Your Garage Or Even in the Clouds!

13

Your Platforms … Putting It All Together

An Amazing Journey Begins …

Introduction

"Be awesome! Be a book nut!"
Dr. Seuss

Good for you … there's a book in you. Have you set its stage … its foundation … its Platform? How about you? Do you know what your stage … your foundation … your Platform is all about? It will take a Village to build—it doesn't happen overnight and it doesn't happen alone.

Every Village starts with just one person. In the case of authorhood … that person is you. Your Village will grow as you add in the necessary components to each stage of the development of your book. The purpose of **Author YOU** is to probe deeply; to bring out your author within; and to show you how to find and create your Platforms—both the Book and the Author.

You might ask—what is the difference between the two? A fine line—but a critical one … a line that will begin to separate as you continue on your authoring journey. Initially, Book and Author Platforms appear to be one— yet they are not. Don't think of them as inseparable twins. The Author Platform is all about you—your persona, your passion for the art and craft of writing as well as the commitment that you will put into it—your personality is all over it—and yes, your developing brand. The Book Platform is all about the Book—a distinct personality in its own right with its characters and scenes or the answers that it provides to the non-fiction reader.

Some authors are soloists—writing only one book. Others find that books begin to multiply. Sometimes in a series format; for others, new genres open. Your Author Platform will build on your expanding book empire—more confidence comes your way; your reputation as an expert is enhanced; people will seek you out. The Book Empire builds on the title or series of books. The reputation of the quality of writing and information/expertise spreads. It becomes a coveted resource—whether for providing solutions or offering entertainment. You and your building brand has rooted in.

Each book adds to your success journey—and the author must learn along the way that not all books will do as well as others. Yet each one adds to the fabric of the author, enabling her or him to stretch their Platforms and audiences.

The Village that adds to your Platform stage will be all the players who bring your book to the reader including editors, designers, illustrators, printers, eBook designers and publishing consultants. Your Village will most likely have a variety of them—but you—your Vision, your Passion and your Commitment will be the driving force. You are the Mayor of that Village—the final decision maker.

I promise ... there will be times when you feel out of synch with work, life, family, book, even self. It's the authoring life. It is sometimes so exciting, you can barely contain yourself: you've created a Rock Star chapter. At other times, so lonely, that you would do anything, even to having Wilson the volley ball to talk to as Tom Hanks did in the movie, *Castaway*. The chapter that you wrote, the one that you thought was the cat's meow, turns out to have a tad of sour milk in it with the second read-through.

My goal is to guide you through these stages as you create your Platforms. In authoring and publishing, it can be the development of your brand; the presentation of the cover and layout; the nuance of a phrase;

the display of your takeaways and must-know-this to the reader; the unique illustrations; the use of stories—it can be a number of things that IDs you to your reader ... your crowd ... your fans.

Your Platforms will always begin with some type of Statement of Fact—why you wrote this book; why you are the author for it; why you are committed to it and its theme/topic; and what value you bring. You do it with Confidence, Clarity, Competence and Commitment. It looks like this:

The Author and Book Platforms ... you can't be successful in your publishing journey without them. Your Author and Book essence, the core infrastructure to build your success upon.

1

Platform Prepping

In the Beginning …

"Wait until you are hungry to say something,
until there is an aching in you to speak."

Natalie Goldberg

Building your Platforms requires you to look in the mirror and ask several questions. Here are yours:

Activity 1

Beginning Your Platform Awareness

What separates you from other authors—is it your experience, travel, job, training ... what?

_____

_____

_____

_____

_____

_____

_____

_____

What are you good at? Are you considered an expert in anything?

_____

_____

_____

_____

Do you have part or fulltime work (or savings/investments) that generates more than enough cash flow to exceed your expenses, allowing you to write and market your book? If no, how are you going to find time to write or finance it?

_____

_____

_____

_____

Are you known as the "go to" person to solve a problem or to consult with for others? Why?

_____

_____

_____

_____

Or, do you feel/see that you are "still in the pack" and haven't broken out? Why?

_____

_____

_____

_____

Have you told anyone about what separates you from the pack? How and When?

_____

_____

_____

_____

Have you written about it in another publication or in articles? Where?

_____

_____

_____

_____

Reading **Author YOU: Creating and Building the Author and Book Platform** and integrating the **Author YOU Model** will create a *significant advantage* over other authors who use the hit-and-miss method for their book journey.

Have you done any branding on yourself? How, When, Where?

Branding on myself?

website

blog

media — more here

Does the world know where, and how to find you ... easily? How?

Do you know what a Platform is? And so you think you have one? Explain.

_____

_____

_____

_____

_____

Do you have a website that immediately "tells" the visitor who you are, what your expertise is and how they can contact you? What is it?

_____

_____

_____

_____

_____

If yes, is your website unique or does it need some work? Do you love the colors? The presentation? Is it easy to navigate—can the visitor find info easily? When the visitor comes to it, does he or she immediately know what you do? If you had a magic wand, what would you change about it?

_____

_____

_____

_____

Would you like to create a book merely as a business card—one that you have available via your website and listing on Amazon, or do you want to create a strategy to sell it?

_____

_____

_____

_____

If your objective is to sell books—lots of them, then what's your game plan to do that?

_____

_____

_____

_____

_____

Do you know the differences between traditional, self and independent publishing? What are they?

_____

_____

_____

_____

Most authors write (*a good thing*); few get their work professionally edited (*a bad thing*); and fewer still understand the dollars, cents and sense of the publishing game (*another bad thing*).

By using the steps and guides on the roadmap included throughout this guidebook in your hands, you move into the top tier of authors.

You gain author power and presence ... and success ... the success that you seek, as you, and only you define it.

Do you know what options, strategies, or ways you have to publish? If yes, which feels right to you?

_____

_____

_____

_____

Do you know what the options cost for any of the ones you know about? What's your guesstimate?

_____

_____

_____

_____

Do you have the time to commit to writing a book? What do you think it will take?

_____

_____

_____

_____

Do you have the time, and moxie, to commit to positioning and selling a book once it's written and published?

_____

_____

_____

_____

Have you ever thought about your Author or Book Platform?
Creating one builds the infrastructure of your book.
What steps do you think you need to do to build that presence?

_____

_____

_____

_____

_____

_____

_____

Smart Authors

Become Savvy

Positioners.

They do it with

✔ Clarity,

✔ Confidence,

✔ Competence

✔ and Commitment.

Being positive is an attitude ... and it needs to be yours.

There are no magic formulas or short cuts to being a successful author—no matter what the latest webinar, teleseminar or hype you hear. It takes work.

Being positive, versus being a sour puss, will open a lot more doors to your success though—think of it as a self-development program. Being positive starts with the determination and willingness to make the effort, and then allowing that effort to feed on it.

With a positive attitude, you can assess who and what you are. You can envision where your Book will be. It's an exciting journey you are beginning ... bringing the right attitude baggage will make the difference between an awesome experience vs. one of weariness from this first step.

2

What's in Your Platform?

Finding Your Core Starts Today

"You can't wait for inspiration.
You have to go after it with a club."

Jack London

There is nothing accidental about creating your Platform.

All successful businesses have one.

All successful authors have one.

Their survival and success depends on it.

PICTURE THIS: you have an idea. An idea for a book that is rejected by every major publisher, a book that contains extensive research and interviews. You can feel it in every bone of your body. You know that it's a break-out ... a leap in your speaking career and a potential best-seller. Do you scrap it ... or do you keep pushing, because in your heart-of-hearts, you know it's big?

That's where I was in late 1986—just coming through an embezzlement that personally cost me in excess of one million dollars, a health crisis and a challenge to my company. I had an idea ... I had completed the work for my dissertation; had completed over 300 one-on-one interviews with women; and had begun writing the commercial book ... a book that hadn't been written on the topic I was immersed in. Painfully.

The topic, I was passionate about. I had a vision for the path it would take me on. I was committed in time, energy and money to make it happen. It was the 28 rejections that created a bit of a road block along the way. Everything from, "It doesn't fit our list," to "No media will ever cover this type of topic," to feminist Gloria Steinem telling me, "Don't write about this ... don't publish this," over dinner one evening at a conference we were both speaking at in Milwaukee.

"But Gloria, *Ms magazine* went under because of the backstabbing and undermining of your female staff ... according to my sources—friends of yours," I responded.

Looking at me, she simply said, "Yes, but it's just not good to talk about this ..."

"Au contraire," I responded. "Don't you see ... if you keep sweeping it under the doormat, how can it be addressed ... much less resolved?"

She finally agreed with me, but felt that using a sledge hammer approach—publishing a form of a manifesto—was too heavy. I could only laugh—this was the woman who had flung more than her share of sledge hammers in her wake-up quest to women and independence cautioning me!

That topic was women and sabotage. Or specifically, why women undermine other women and how to change it. A taboo topic ... one that no one was speaking on and certainly no one was writing about. My niche to be.

Not knowing a lick about self-publishing (outside of it meaning vanity press—a taboo for "legit" authors), I sold the book to a small New York press, ignoring the advice of all but my agent who told me to ... he believed in the book as well.

I sold the book to a small New York press, ignoring the advice of all but my agent who told me to ... he believed in the book as well.

Got Platform?

If you plan to write a book; to use it for marketing your expertise; a Platform you need. I had a Platform in the 80s, it just wasn't called that back then.

The Author and Book Platforms consist of three key areas: *Passion, Vision* and *Commitment*. Think of it as a funnel with three balls. Each is connected to the author as they flow through the neck. While within the funnel, they are tossed about as the book is getting ready for birth. The fourth area that comes into play is *People*—they will find you through your channels of *Passion, Vision* and *Commitment*.

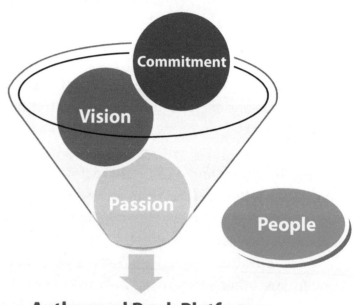

Author and Book Platforms

With the Internet, many believe that the Platform is all about the people you are connected with. Granted, you've got to have people to buy your books—but the three factors of *Passion, Vision* and *Commitment* are essential. *People* won't care about you or your book if you don't have them.

One of the most successful ad campaigns of recent years has been the one created by Capital One credit cards: *What's in your wallet?* To morph that phrase just a tad: *What's in your Platform? For you, the Author, and for your Book?*

Activity 2

Finding Your Author Platform

Get out your pen or pencil. To get to the core of your Author Platform, it's important to answer the following questions:

What's your Intention as an Author? Is it to be a "best-selling" author? Is it making lots of money—and what does "lots" mean to you? Is your intent to have celebrity or notoriety as an author? Is it designed to position you as the "go-to" or expert in your field? Is it to become a sought-after, paid speaker? What is it?

_____

_____

_____

_____

_____

_____

_____

What is important to you? Integrity as an author, for example? Or are you known for your clarity of expression perhaps?

_____

_____

_____

_____

You will be working with many people as you develop—or grow —"your baby."
What trust levels are important for others with whom you will and must work?

_____

_____

_____

_____

What do you feel passionate about when you think of your writing and your book?

_____

_____

_____

_____

How much time will you commit to writing your book?

_____

_____

_____

_____

How much time will you commit to marketing your book?

_____

_____

_____

_____

How much money will you commit to creating, publishing and marketing your book?

_____

_____

_____

_____

What time factor—constraints—do you work under in your life ... at work, at play, for yourself?

_____

_____

_____

_____

_____

What inspires you?

_____

_____

_____

_____

What does Author Success mean to you?

_____

_____

_____

_____

_____

_____

_____

_____

Activity 3

Finding Your Book Platform

Continuing, it's time to look closely at the book you are creating. To get to the core of your Book Platform, answer these questions:

What would your book look like if you concentrated on your Passion?

_____

_____

_____

_____

_____

_____

_____

What is your Intention for your book? Is it marketing a Product to create money, sans the craft of creating it? Is its intent to make you a Celebrity? Is it part of a series or franchise of other books you've created? Is it designed to be positioned as a benchmark in an industry or area as a contribution to your field? Is your vision to have "trade-marked" types of names, characters, scenarios? What is it?

_____

_____

_____

_____

What is important for your book? Why are you writing it?

_____

_____

_____

_____

If you need to do interviews, surveys or include others in the research/writing of your book, what trust levels are important in working with others?

_____

_____

_____

_____

Are there any topical, political, controversial or newsworthy themes that your book is connected to and with?

_____

_____

_____

What are the key components, characteristics and nuances of your book?

_____

_____

_____

_____

What if turning your Passion into reality became your measure of success ... what does Book Success look like to you?

_____

_____

_____

_____

With confidence ...
anything is possible!

The road to your success as an Author will most likely be cloaked with detours—some with unbelievable potholes—and some with the most amazing experiences and happenings. Your confidence as an Author will be woven with the magic seed: courage. Courage allows you to stick your neck out and position yourself in a controversial topic as *the* expert. Courage allows you to take your creativity into realms you never imagined. Courage allows great ideas and concepts to bubble over.

Courage—your courage—is woven through the Author's fabric and as your words pour forth, your thoughts and ideas are shaped. In them, you, the Author becomes a conduit to the Reader ... taking him or her into a world of opportunity, solutions and dreams.

What an amazing honor we Authors have.

3

The Passion Factor

Ebb and Flow As You Create

"Fill your paper with the breathings of your heart."

William Wordsworth

For you and your book, *Passion* and *Vision* are similar to peanut butter and jelly. Similar in that if you are a devotee of either, you know that they can stand alone or be happily merged with another ingredient. But for the author and book, togetherness is a must. One without the other creates a mediocre outcome.

The Author's Passion Factor

An opera, any opera, without Passion just isn't an opera. You may not understand Italian, but you can sense, you can feel the Passion behind the words and gestures. You know that the singer is driven to convey his or her message as you get caught up … and down with arias and movements. It's all about Passion.

As an author, being passionate about your topic is critical. As it is for your book. Passion is essential—you must care about your topic, your book, your writing. The average book is closed by page 18 … you don't want yours to be. Ask:

- Is your writing engaging?

- If you write fiction, do your characters resonate with the reader?

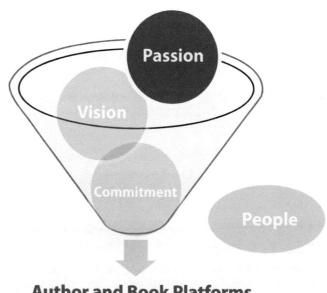

Author and Book Platforms

- If you write non-fiction, do your examples/stories connect with the reader as if you were having a conversation with them?

- Does the reader sense that you care about how they respond to your words?

- When your book is opened, does your reader fall in?

When you have Passion for your topic, it radiates everywhere. In your conversations with friends; from the stage as you speak; in media related interviews. If you participate in book clubs, your fans enthusiastically look forward to meeting you—whether through a local event or via Skype.

My Passion that morphed me away from personal finance, a genre within which I had successfully published two books with traditional publishers and made my living, was seeded from the financial embezzlement I experienced in the 80s—a female partner had withdrawn moneys for her personal drug use from a commercial credit line that I had personally guaranteed. The misuse of the funds only surfaced when all the moneys were gone; little had been paid to the many contractors who had provided building services. I had been duped—I'm not dumb, how did this happen?

Authors and books are no different.

When Passion is in play, you know what the author and book intent are—you can feel it, flow with it—as you weave through the pages that unfold before your eyes.

The Passion of the opera singer is hers ... and it becomes yours as you ebb and flow with it ... just as you want the reader to do with your words.

I had to go back to school in my attempt to unscramble the mess that she and her husband and other partners made. Seeded by the "I'm not dumb, how did I get duped?" nudge, I started looking at women and their workplace relationships. I read ... and I wrote papers as I worked through the course work for my doctorate in business. I was clueless at that time as to what the Vision for all my work was ... besides survival ... but I was passionate about the topic I was probing and, of course, survival. And I was ready to start putting it all together.

That incidence started me on a path that led to multiple books, speaking engagements, consulting contracts and corporate spokesperson positions over a 25-year period. I became the "go-to" person if there was toxicity and conflict in the health care workplace.

Working with the theme of women sabotaging other women—what the problem is; its causation, the effect and finally, the solution. I created a career quest that spanned three plus decades. With a total of six books on the topic, being identified as a pioneer and conducting nine national studies, I'm still as passionate about the topic as I ever was.

It ticks me off when people undermine other people, especially women doing it to other women.

Today, I have a new Passion—one that was rooted with my first book that was published in 1981, *The Woman's Guide to Financial Savvy*. This was pre-embezzlement, where my time, energy and career were devoted to financial planning. I was passionate about educating women to make right money choices and I did have a Vision for where I wanted to go, but I was clueless as to the time and energy needed to make that happen.

Authoring and publishing was seeded one night. After dinner with a well-known national columnist and author, he took/used some of my ideas in a column that he published, and was paid for. I was not. My take away aha: if I didn't start taking and using my own ideas, others would ... and publish them.

My first book, *The Woman's Guide to Financial Savvy* was published by St. Martin's Press in 1981. That has led to 30 additional books and counting. My journey has taken me from publishing with the big New York houses, the big agents, to creating my own imprint.

Authors come to the authoring
party from different routes.
Rarely are the routes the same ...
what connects you with other
authors is that you each heard
the *Publishing Siren* ...
and you responded to it.

As with most seeds, there is hope of great things. My only *vision* was to create a book that was desired and helpful to women—that's a *"V"* that is lower-cased. I did, and I thought it would be the only book I wrote—my vision never saw multiple books, so it was quite limited in retrospect. Along the publishing path, as more books were "booked," I became book publishing smart. Mistakes and mishaps with publishers along the way added to my smartness. Others asked me to tell them—show them about publishing. By the time I had created my own publishing imprint after publishing over a dozen books with traditional publishers, I had plenty to say, tell and show.

The seed grew; it was fertilized and watered. Today, my Passion is all about publishing—a field that is changing as quickly as the world turns. Helping authors publish quality books is rewarding; keeping them away from the publishing predators is something that I celebrate; enjoying their success with sales and connecting with their new found fans is intoxicating. Who wouldn't love it?

For you, the *Passion Factor* is as critical as breathing. If you don't have it from the get-go, your book will never develop the roots it needs to survive and thrive. Acquiring usually comes from curiosity or an event that triggers a quest, such as what happened to me.

Beware of Predators

Activity 4

What's in Your Heart of Hearts?

Why do people publish a book? Why do authors write them? The reasons are numerous and you probably need all your fingers and toes cleared to count the ways. For you as the author, it's time to ask, and answer:

In your heart of hearts, why are you attracted to the topic of your book?

_____

_____

_____

_____

_____

_____

In your heart of hearts, why are you writing this book?

_____

_____

_____

_____

**Do you come away re-charged and enthusiastic after sharing with others what you are doing?
How does it make you feel?**

_____

_____

_____

_____

Summing up why you should be passionate and care about your book, it would be:

_____

_____

_____

For your book, ask and answer:

Does your book solve a problem, provide a new solution, even to a topic that has been written and published before? How?

_____

_____

_____

When you tell others about your book's topic, do they get excited? Do they want a copy now? Do they tell you that they wished they had had your book years ago? What is it and how do they express their comments?

_____

_____

_____

_____

Summing up why others should be passionate and care about your book, it would be:

_____

_____

_____

_____

Perfection may be the Author's worst enemy..

Publishing is an amazing journey, loaded with unbelievable zigzags, detours and paths. Interesting. They just may be the most direct route you take to get your book completed. If your objective is to create the "perfect" book, your journey may continue in perpetuity—a never ending one that leaves you, the Author in you, and your circle of supporters frustrated. Your Passion for the topic, your Book, may slowly dissipate.

Perfection is the enemy of the good … and your book could just the next great thing … if you will just let it out. Guaranteed, there will be changes you will want to make. Those dang missing typos that creep in and some late-breaking story that you want to add. You can …it's called "next."

4

The Vision Factor

See It and It will Come

"For my part I know nothing with any certainty,
but the sight of the stars makes me dream."

Vincent van Gogh

Your Platforms continue with *Vision*—what the author—you—visualize and feel is the big picture. For you, and for your book. Within your *Vision*, your ideas formulate, they take root and embrace all the "what ifs" that can come your way. Where do you see your book taking you? Where do you see taking your book? What does it look like? Does your book have a "look" to it—for both the cover and interior design?

What and Who is your audience? If you think "everyone," you will get lost in the crowd. The Niche Factor is powerful—narrow whom your book is for, where a smaller crowd can find you as you reach out as the expert/go-to person.

When Woman to Woman: From Sabotage to Support was initially published in 1987, I thought it was for every working woman. Wrong. No book is for everyone. The belief that it was came from naiveté on my part—it was part of my *Vision*. I knew there was a problem; I understood what the emotional, physical and financial effects were for the working women—I thought that all women would also see *my Vision.* Wrong ... and incredibly naïve.

I thought it was ideal for the general workplace. Wrong. Corporate America was scared to death of the topic—women undermining women? You've got to be kidding! I had conducted a national study that included several thousand men and women; interviewed and listened to hundreds of painful stories of betrayal; and discovered that productivity and turnover were directly related ... surely corporate America wanted the message.

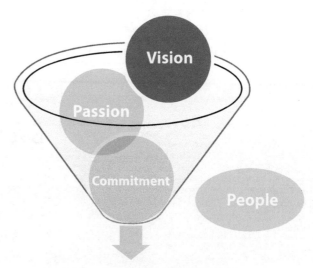

Author and Book Platforms

Wrong, wrong and more wrong. It was a hot potato—gender harassment topics were forbidden—women undermining and harassing women; sexual harassment topics—men harassing women—were in.

I thought that the mainstream media would embrace it. I was right. *Oprah* loved it. So did the *CNN, Donahue, Sally, Geraldo* and every other first name host along with the *Wall Street Journal, People* magazine, *Time, Newsweek, USA Today*, local press, radio and TV across the county. Even the *National Enquirer. Woman to Woman* was a publicist's dream. Hot potato.

After the first *Oprah* appearance, my offices received a call from another author's office in my city at that time—Tom Peters' personal assistant. She had heard about the book ... the women in his office were driving him nuts with the backstabbing and gossiping. Could I come in and talk with them ... and bring a copy of the *Oprah* show? I did.

Not surprising, he was leery of the topic—the hot potato factor—and too hot for the corporate workplace for him to openly endorse ... but would I help with his office problem? Yes, I would.

It wasn't until several Directors of Nursing heard me speak on the topic that I found the "right" corporate workplace: health care. Not every-woman. Rather, a female-dominated workplace: health care. The field of nursing was a viper's den of undermining and toxicity. The snakes and all their kin flourished within it. The first book specifically for health care, *The Briles Report on Women in Health Care*, was birthed in 1993 and became a selection for the Nurse's Book Society and a best seller within it.

A few years later, *Zapping Conflict in the Health Care Workplace* debuted as the main selection and enjoyed thousands of sales and multiple orders. Later books on the topic were specifically written for the health care field with the latest in 2009: *Stabotage! How to Deal with the Pit Bulls, Skunks, Snakes, Scorpions and Slugs in the Health Care Workplace*.

*Niche your book.
It is so much easier to
be the whale in the lake
versus the sardine
in the sea.*

I had found my niche.
Speaking and book sales skyrocketed.

My Vision was a tad blurred in the beginning of the journey, but with focus, the clarity came through.

Your *Vision* creates the big picture—I saw my book on major shows and covered by the media. It was the first book with a national study of the topic. I saw it used within the corporate workplace—the right workplace had to be discovered. It was. I saw it branding me and my speaking. Taking me to the next level.

Activity 5

Finding Your Vision

What is your Vision for you, the Author?

_____

_____

_____

_____

_____

_____

_____

_____

_____

What could get in your way from creating your author Vision?

_____

_____

_____

_____

_____

_____

_____

_____

Activity 6

Finding Your Book's Vision

What is your Vision for your Book?

_____

_____

_____

_____

_____

_____

_____

_____

_____

What could get in your Book's way from creating your Book's Vision?

_____

_____

_____

_____

_____

_____

_____

_____

_____

Authors should be willing to break the rules.

Let's face it … doing the same old, same old is downright boring. And, it's equivalent to inhaling your own exhaust. When you do, you risk stifling your creativity and eliminating your sense of wonder … your sense of going into a realm that just may open up unbelievable and rewarding outcomes.

Just because an author you admire gets up every morning and writes from four to seven doesn't mean you have to—mornings may not be your thing. Just because a panel you heard of authors say they write a minimum of two hours a day doesn't mean you have to—you may be a Binger … writing a full chapter in one sitting. Just because the latest hot author says she only does eBooks doesn't mean that's your solo platform … your audience may need print books, as well as eBooks, audio books and workbooks.

Rule breaking can be fun and quite liberating—it can be part of your Vision as you enter new territory and became the Book pioneer you envision yourself as. Try it, you just may like it!

5

The Commitment Factor

If You Don't Commit, You and Your Book Won't Fit

"For my part I know nothing with any certainty,
but the sight of the stars makes me dream."
Vincent van Gogh

Ahhh ... *Commitment* is the "black hole" for many. Too, too many. You can have all the Passion and Vision, but if you aren't Committed ... you will fail. Period.

There were plenty of times when I wanted to toss in the towel ... and there have been a few times when I've aborted a book—doing a reassessment of my Platforms—always, always asking: is this a right fit for me; do I have the same Passion I had for it as I did when the idea was first seeded; do I see the Vision as big as I initially did; and do I have the Commitment of time, energy and money to support this new offspring?

Interestingly, an idea that I had created a national survey for in 90s; done a full proposal; written a few chapters; and started one-on-one interviews was put aside. Why? Because after doing a Passion, Vision, Commitment assessment of the book project, I determined that I was too ahead of my time for it.

Twenty-five years later, across from me was a new Book Shepherding client who now shared the same Vision and Passion I had from years past. Amazingly, we had both given it the same title! And I knew it was time to pass my pen to another.

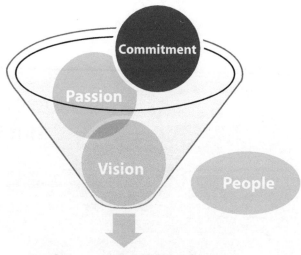

Eagerly, I shared all my original work and "gifted" it to her. It was time. I still had the Passion and Vision for the topic, but I didn't have the Commitment. She did. She was stunned when she got my email with my original work. I was thrilled to find a "home" for it and looked forward to working with her over the next several months as the book, her book, evolves.

Author and Book Platforms

Commitment means time, energy and money.
Nothing more, nothing less. It's a BIG "nothing."

How much time will you put into supporting your book? Writing a quality book is just one segment of the commitment triangle. It's what you do with it as it comes out of the gate; and it is truly a race, in competition with an immense field. Speakers should aggressively pre-market within the year prior to publication—letting their contacts know that "the book is coming" and that special speaking discounts will be tied to the launch. My entire speaking calendar was booked ahead for a solid year with the announcement of a new book—which meant I was busy, many thousands of books would be sold and that my *brand*—"Dr. Judith Briles, expert in toxic behavior in female dominated workplaces"—was solid.

You, the author, must carve out time to support this new child of yours.
You must create the time to connect with People—your fans, clients, crowd,
tribe, readers—whatever category they fit into; to connect with the media;
to write articles. And you must create the time to work the appropriate
social media channels. This is your business of being an author.

And this is your work ... work that will lead to building your brand and your career. The reason that I landed a cover story in *People* magazine, on *Oprah, CNN,* the *Wall Street Journal* and over 1,000 media related events was that I made the time for it. Not a paid publicist ... just me ... working the phones, making the connections, following up and booking a slot. Just me and the ingredient of time, along with my Vision and Passion.

How much energy will you put into supporting your book? "Lots" would be an excellent response. No doubt your Vision and Passion will be the driving forces. Plus the factor of money—you have an investment that you want to see a return on. The return can come quickly, or it can evolve over a period of time. Days, and evenings, will be long. If there ever was a time to take care of you, this is it. Doing any type of media can have you up in the middle of the night being bubbly, insightful and enthusiastic—yet your body is saying, "Hey, I want to be prone ..."

Fueling your energy demands that you be selective with where and what you put it into. Two of my long-time **Keepers** (you'll see these Keepers throughout) that I encourage you to use are:

Don't do well what you have no business doing.

If you never say "no," your "yeses" are worthless.

Knowing your audience—what your niche is—will help define where your energy should be directed.

If it isn't a fit, don't commit to putting your time in. No exceptions.

How much money will you put into supporting your book? Stories abound about how an author was down to his last $5 on a credit line before the big sale came in ... you don't have to live that dream ... or nightmare. Books do take money—the creation could be many thousands of dollars.

As *The Book Shepherd*, putting together the book budget is the first thing I do in my offices with a new client. As the author, you are creating a product—a product that could launch, or re-launch, an amazing journey that can last decades. How much are you willing to invest to get you there?

Pre-publication costs include editing, design of cover and interior, printing, ISBN numbers—and possibly consulting with an expert, such as book shepherd or book/writing coach or even a ghost writer (you may be the author but writing may not be your skill, your gift). Then comes warehousing and fulfillment if you plan to reach out to other marketing avenues; avenues outside of back-of-the-room sales. Publicity, marketing and social media strategists may also be engaged.

All cost money. Be realistic ... my books and speaking have grown and fed a family, built a house and have been my primary support for over 30 years. None of it was done on a penny. No one gave me anything. With the combination of speaking and books, money was always there to add fuel to the expanding book empire. Its growth came from having a book budget and spending plan. What's critical is for you to be realistic from the get-go.

Judith's Visual Game Plan for Platform Building for Stabotage!

The next two pages will introduce you to one of the stages I go through when I'm in the "book creation" mode. This one deals with the GameBoard, will I layout on the wall a visual of all the things that will involve the book—in this case *Stabotage! How to Deal with the Pit Bulls, Skunks, Snakes, Scorpions & Slugs in the Health Care Workplace*. Later, you will see how I start the layout for a few of the chapters.

The GameBoard kick-starts the massive organization for the team needed; gets me focused on what I'm writing about and who my reader is along with the benefits they will receive from the book. Areas of expenses and revenues are also identified.

Supplies to have: Lots of sticky notes or PostIts®, poster paper or a good size white board, treats/rewards of your choice—I will have miscellaneous notes that will augment 10 key areas that I will then post on the Game Plan to put on the notes as the Board builds out. Sometimes "reminders/notes" and some of my favorite "Keepers" are added.

They will include—

People: Who am I writing for?—in *Stabotage!*, that would have been anyone who worked within the health care industry.

Outlets: What form am I going to produce the book in?

Significance and Value Provided: I had to specifically identify the problem—toxic behavior in the workplace and create some solutions for conflict resolution. What do I need to include and what methods will be ID'd to deal with it?

Staying Connected: How would I stay connected with my clients and readers—I need to have a few ways—both traditionally and using the Internet?

Joint Venture Partners: Who were my cheerleaders—fans—who would let others in the health care community know of the new book coming along and recommend me to speak about it?

Income: Authors want revenues—where were mine going to come from?

Key Resources: Who will I need on my publishing team to create the book?

Outlays: What will I have to spend money on to create the book; to support it when it's birthed; marketing efforts; thank-you gifts; speaking gig support, etc.?

Key Activities: What things do I need to do to bring in money, support me, marketing, etc.?

DumpZone: A critical part of the Game Plan—what areas should I not venture down, attempt to partner with or just not do?

Judith's Visual Game Plan for Platform

Book title: Stabotage! How to deal with the pit bulls, skunks, snakes, scorpions & slugs in the health care workplace

People

Have Conflict
Work in Healthcare
Nurses
Women
Managers-Directors
Nurse Associations
Hospital Associations

Outlets

Print
eBook
CD-DVD

Significance and Value Provided

Conflict resolution
Better communication
Quizzes to ID Staboteur
New Script to Delete Conflict
Fun
Problem solving
Based on Nat'l Survey

Staying Connected

New website
Newsletter
Blog
FB page
YouTube
Radio show?
Give free articles to all HC mags
and newsletters

Note to JB —
If you Never say
NO, your YESES
are worthless!!!

Income

Book sales via speaking-single
Book sales via Premium sales
Stuff: T-shirts, Buttons,
Bookmarks
Book clubs
Paid gigs
Speaking at hospitals

Income

Speaking at nursing
conferences
Consulting
Webinars
Create HC Cruise
Sponsors for gigs
Sponsored book signs

Joint Venture Partners

Jo, Dianne, Leslie, Karyn
HC Assns Meeting Planners
Hospitals
Nursing Assns

Key Resources:

Cover: Rebecca
Interior: Ronnie
Illustrator: Shannon
Indexer: John
Editor: John
Printer: Cameron
Readers
Survey takers
Interviewees
Endorsers
Nurse Cruise

Outlays

$$$:
Flyer for book sales special
Exhibiting
Buttons-promo for
   Exhibits
Special Flyer for each gig
Pay for JM to attend
   all gigs

Outlays

Speaking Kits
Media Kits
Books for promo
Books to Assoc mags
   for reviews
Thank you gifts
% of back sales back
Muse Kickstart:
   Cruise to start writing

Outlays

JB time:
20 hours/week
   to market
Massage weekly
Create articles
3 days for each gig

JB's Muse
Water, water, water

Key Activities

PostCard Campaign
PT Marketing Director-Dolores
Exhibiting where JB speaks
Newsletter for Marketing to HC
Reward: M&Ms!!
Subscribe to Nursing-Hospital
   mags
Regular Articles for HC Assoc.
   mags
Get Sponsor

CRUISE!

DumpZone

High % Male Groups
Speaking Bureaus
Corporations
Teachers
Exhibiting Where JB doesn't Speak
Unsponsored Book Signings
Saying Yes to All

Note to JB –
Don't do well
what you have
NO business doing!!

Note to JB –
Don't speak where you
don't feel passion about
the group and/or feel
that there are people in
the audience who
can hire you ...
EVER!!!

Activity 7
Finding Your Commitment Factor

Let's review the earlier questions and now answer them fully.

How much *Time* will you put into supporting your book?

_____

_____

_____

_____

_____

_____

_____

_____

How much of your *Energy* will you put into supporting your book?

_____

_____

_____

_____

In what *Areas* will you direct your energy to support your book?

_____

_____

_____

_____

How much *Money* will you put into supporting your book?

_____

_____

_____

_____

_____

What could *get* in your way from you supporting your book?

_____

_____

_____

_____

Activity 8

Finding the Time

How much *Time* do you think your book will need to get it off the ground?

_____

_____

_____

_____

_____

_____

_____

_____

_____

_____

How much of your *Energy* do you think your book needs to be successful?

_____

_____

_____

_____

How much *Money* do you think your book will need to get its message out?

_____

_____

_____

_____

Have you *put* together a financial budget to support your book?

_____

_____

_____

_____

What *is* it and in what areas will you direct your money?

_____

_____

_____

_____

_____

Activity 9
Finding Your Financial Commitment to Your Book

It's amazing how so few authors really know what their unit (book) cost is. Totaling the moneys that you spend for design—cover and interior—along with printing, shipping, editing, or any consultants you've worked within the creation process, you will come up with a sum.

Take that amount, divide by the price of your book (if you know it now or estimate what it will be), and you come up with how many books you need to sell to "break even." Just knowing that number—how many books you need to sell to recoup costs—can take a great deal of pressure off your shoulders.

You may have 2,000 books in inventory. If your break-even comes in at 500 books, it's amazing the mental relief it is to many an author to know that they only have to move/sell 500 books to get their initial money back. The next book sale starts the profit train.

This Activity is designed to crunch your numbers. Savvy authors know what the cost is for creating their book. No, you don't get to factor in your time—that's your creative, equity commitment. The Miscellaneous category could include the cost of your ISBN; packaging material for fulfillment or sending books for reviews; costs related to starting your publishing company; or website or social media related strategies.

The Total Cost of My Book Is:

Title _____

Number of Copies Printed _____

Cost of Cover _____

Cost of Editing _____

Cost of Layout _____

Cost of Art/Illustrations _____

Cost of Printing _____

Cost of Shipping _____

Cost of Consultants _____

Cost of Website _____

Cost of Marketing _____

Miscellaneous _____

Other _____

Other _____

Total Cost of Publishing: _____

The Cost of Each Book Is:

To determine your cost per book, divide the total cost of publishing by the number of books printed. The result is your cost per book.

$$\text{Cost per book} = \frac{\text{Total Cost of Publishing}}{\text{\# of Books Printed}}$$

When you have your Cost of Publishing, divide it by the number of books you are Printing and insert below. If you are only doing an eBook run, then you will still have a cost of creating it. Determine the number of eBooks you need to sell—most likely, they will only be a few hundred dollars.

My cost is: $_____

In most cases, publishers will take just the cost paid for printing and divide it by the number of books printed—they figure that the cover, layout, editing, etc., is spread (or amortized) over the life and total number of books printed.

The Breakeven Number of Books to Sell Is:

To determine breakeven number to recoup your publishing costs, divide your total cost of publishing by the price of the book. The result is the number of books you need to sell to recover your initial moneys.
The formula below assumes you sell at full price. If it's discounted and sold through retailers or wholesalers (such as Amazon or a bookstore), the number needed to be sold will approximately double.

Breakeven # of Books to Sell (B) = Cost of Publishing (C)
                                     Price of Book (P)

When you have your cost of publishing and know the price of your book, determine your Breakeven and insert below. If you are only doing an eBook run, then you will still have a cost of creating and publishing it. Determine the number of eBooks you need to sell to Breakeven.

My Breakeven is: total cost of book is (C) =_____

C divided by P = # of books you have to sell

Know the cost of your book.

Failure is not the end ...
it's the beginning.

Few authors come out of the Book Creation Zone with a blatant, hands-down, no work to it successful Book. The truth is, we do a lot of stumbling. We make mistakes. Sometimes getting into the wrong Village and engaging the wrong people to work with. Sometimes spending money for the wrong thing. Sometimes just not doing our homework.

Gulp, sometimes we get so derailed that we need to re-commit to our Book and to ourselves as the Author.

Whatever the detour or barrier is, it's not fatal. It becomes part of the learning curve that will take you to the next, next level—closer to success.

6

The People Factor

IDing Your Fans, Buyers and Community

"Keep away from people who try to belittle your
ambitions. Small people always do that, but the really
great make you feel that you, too, can become great."

Mark Twain

Build it and they will come is the belief of many. Maybe. Maybe not. Most likely, not. My first book, *The Woman's Guide to Financial Savvy*, was published in 1981 the old fashioned way—with a New York publishing house courting me and doing it up big. Three printings in three weeks, national TV appearances including *Good Morning America*—it was exciting and successful.

Times have changed with the Internet now being a driving force—and that's a good thing. Authors can take control; reach far more people within their niche instantaneously. They don't need the New York houses and, in fact, few care who you publish with. What they want to know includes:

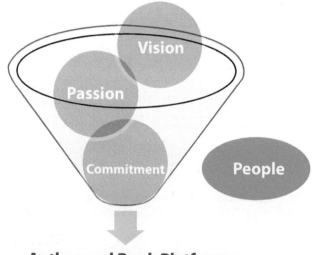

Author and Book Platforms

- Does your book solve their pain or provide a solution?

- Does it entertain or amuse?

- If a printed book, is it quality, or does it look like crap (which too many do)?

- If an eBook, has the layout been carefully "laid out" versus just dumped in a Word document and hoping for the best?

What authors need is a *Game Plan* that is directly tied to the marketing of their book to the people that it is for. When you have Passion, Vision and Commitment, the People will come. Build it so they can find you. Reach out to them so they know you are there.

Activity 10

Finding Your People

What can you do to reach your audience, crowd and fans to reach your breakeven number?

_____

_____

_____

_____

In 2011, approximately 3,000,000 books of all types were created—most likely, 2,700,000 shouldn't have been.

Passion, Vision and Commitment will keep you out of the trash heap.

Activity 11

Who Are Your People?

In Person:

_____

_____

_____

_____

_____

_____

_____

_____

_____

_____

On the Internet:

_____

_____

_____

_____

_____

_____

_____

_____

_____

_____

Other Venues:

_____

_____

_____

_____

On Twitter:

_____

_____

_____

_____

_____

_____

On LinkedIn:

On Facebook:

_____

_____

_____

_____

_____

_____

_____

_____

_____

On Google+:

_____

_____

_____

_____

_____

On Pinterest:

_____

_____

_____

_____

On YouTube:

_____

_____

_____

_____

_____

On your Blog(s):

_____

_____

_____

_____

Activity 12

What Name(s) Will You Use for You, the Author, and Your Book?

How do you want to brand yourself—your topic? Are you going to use just your name? A unique phrase? Your book title? What?

On Twitter:

_____

_____

_____

_____

_____

On LinkedIn:

_____

_____

_____

_____

_____

On Facebook:

_____

_____

_____

_____

_____

On Pinterest:

_____

_____

_____

_____

On Google+:

_____

_____

_____

_____

On YouTube:

_____

_____

_____

_____

Your Blog(s):

_____

_____

_____

_____

_____

_____

See it. Build it. Find them. Tell them ... and they will come.

There's a reason that most authors sell only a few hundred copies of their book, if that. Savvy authors know that they don't wait for book buyers to knock on their door and call them out of the blue. They have to find them and connect.

The Internet has billions of users. There are more than the typical author's few hundred buyers. As you learn how to reach out, offer information that will solve problems, provide solutions, inspire, entertain—whatever your book is intended to do, the Reader ... your Book buyer ... will come. It's an awesome experience.

Finding your people, the ones that are open to your ideas, believe in your concepts and become your fans will not only sell books, but will add energy back to you. It's an honor and a thrill for Authors to sign their books for another, to look them in the eye and say, "Thank you ..."

7

Keeping Your Platform on the Right Track

Book Mapping Can Lead the Way

"Writing a novel is like driving a car at night.
You can see only as far as your headlights,
but you can make the whole trip that way."

E.L. Doctorow

Are you confident with the Platforms you are developing? Do they have the clarity that matches your Vision? Are you Committed? Is your Platform created to take the conception of your book to its publishing delivery? And then to carry it from the delivery stage to adulthood success?

More times than not, most authors haven't really thought through the various stages of their book. Some are in the beginning stages of writing; many are in the midst of their manuscripts; and others are in the final stages of completion, ready for editing, layout, cover design and anything else the manuscript needs before being sent to the printer. Few have really thought about what they are going to do when they have actual book in hand. You must.

Welcome to my Game Plan Design Board ...

Join me on the journey I traveled through as I created my book published in 2009, *Stabotage: How to Deal with the Pit Bulls, Skunks, Snakes, Scorpions & Snakes in the Health Care Workplace.* Since then, it's enjoyed five printings and is used globally in health care communities, which is great fun for this author!

I will share the layouts that I did on my Game Plan for the first few chapters of the book which book interior designer Nick Zelinger has re-created from my cryptic notes. I'm a highly visual person—so I'm one of those that needs EVERYTHING out so I can see what I'm working with—if

anything gets put away ... it's an out of sight, out of mind experience for me. File cabinets are not my friend when I'm actually writing a book. When a book was in process, all files and support material were visable and easily accessed.

What Works for Me ...

I freely use multiple colors of sticky notes to cue me in for topics and areas. And I freely move them about—re-arranging chapters, topics and whatever else I put on them as ideas came into mind. As I got into the book, a significant amount of interviews were used throughout to support or make a point that I was presenting. Voices. Believe me, some were quite painful to hear them retell. Sometimes I was interviewing them for one chapter within the book and they would share a thought that I knew belonged in another—a new sticky note was made to add that to that section. The notes weren't detailed—they served as "ticklers."

Rewards work for me. This book was written around M&Ms—when I finished a chapter, I got a bag. If I was really stuck ... well ... I got a few then too! Cheetos are another guilty vice (I know, I know—there is no nutritional value ... and gads, what an orange mess on the keyboard). And truth be told, there were times that I was so into a chapter that I would tell myself that I got to pee if I would just finish this section—an author has to do what she has to do!

Oh ... and no one is allowed into my space—friends, my cleaning guy, even hubby—nobody.

What works for me, may not for you ... but I've found that when you see, hear, experience how other authors pull their books together, it opens up "ahas" and possibilities that just might be the door waiting to be opened.

Judith's Game Plan Design Board for "Stabotage!"

Chapter 2
Survey Speaks

#337
respondent's
quote

Key Questions

Is Stabotage in WP?
Left job because
of it?
Has it inc/dec in
past 5 years?
Who created?
What was gender?

Key Results

Stabotage in
Workplace?
YES: 55%
Left job: 51%
Increase?: 56%

Who creates?
  Manager: 63%

3217 respondents:
93% female;
46# staff;
54# management

Define Stabotage

Who's Who

$$$ costs

ID Pit Bulls
at work

Pit Bulls, Snakes,
Scorpions, Skunks,
Slugs

Add stories,
descriptions,
behaviors-how
to deal w/

JB's Keeper

Losing $_____
  per year

Activity 13

The 4 Ps—
Pitch, Plan,
People and
Platform

When I work with authors in creating their Platforms, there are other "Ps" that enter the scene beside the necessary ingredient of People. They are Plan and Pitch. Questions for you at this stage include:

1. Do you have a following that will support your book and that will create book sales and begin the buzz building ... the People part of your Platform?

_____

_____

2. How do you Plan on selling your book?

_____

_____

_____

_____

3. How do you plan on getting the People to come to You and your Book?

_____

_____

_____

_____

4. What Pitch (or hook) are you going to use to entice book buyers and the various components of media opportunities?

_____

_____

_____

_____

Judith's Game Plan Design Board for "Stabotage!"

Chapter 3
Pit Bulls, Snakes,
Scorpions,
Skunks, Slugs

Bette Davis
quote:
"All About Eve"

Add stories,
descriptions,
behaviors-how
to deal w/

Unique factors
in female
Workplace

Nurse Abby story

Domino

Discrimination

Covert

ID Staboteur
in Midst Quiz

11 Questions
with Answers

Nurses Eat Young

Stats—
Journal Nursing
Mgmt, May 2005

London University
Royal College of
Nursing, 2007

Verbal Abuse

Luther Christman
interview

Helen Cox study,
2007

JB Keepers—
do 2:
Hire Slowly,
Fire Quickly
and Verbal Abuse

JB's Keeper

Summing Up

Too many authors fail by simply believing that if they wrote it, printed it, that they would come. Wrong. You've got to reach out and connect ... you've got to do the work to connect with others and start the buzz machine. Your *Platform,* your *Plan,* your *Pitch* become the foundation for the success of your Book.

Your next questions are:

1. Which Platform is the one that You, and your Book, will succeed with?

_____

_____

_____

_____

_____

_____

_____

_____

2. Which Platform is the one that will lead you to your readers and fans, and them to you?

_____

_____

_____

_____

3. Which is the right Platform for You and your Book?

_____

_____

_____

_____

Judith's Game Plan Design Board for "Stabotage!"

Chapter 4
Why Do These Critters Breed in Your Workplace?

- Madeline Albright quote
- Problem—6 pts
- female dominated Workplace

- big % of women not wanting to work w/ women
- discount of behavioral skills over clinical
- techno resistant workforce
- older employee resentment
- Unions

- Denial Factors
- Cite WW orig study
- Cite Cheslers, Hein, Wiseman, Lamb books
- Social Trends
- stats on corp pay
- Crab Crawl
- Story from MD crab cooker
- Cite interviews for multiples

- Women Eat Young
- Cite Hillary Clinton column, 2008
- Bullier-Bullette
- Interview: Jane Stuart
- Gender Stereotypes 4 pts

- Power
- Complex
- Squeezes
- Patient Misuse
- 10,000++ reported since 2006
- JB's Keepers:
- Summing Up

I've found that putting my authors through a couple of mapping processes reveals an amazing amount of information. The first Activity that provides a treasure chest of information is *Book Mapping*.

I've always used a form of mind-mapping to work through new ideas—be they a book or a project. Let's start with *Book Mapping*. It will reveal the Who, What, Where, Why and How of your book and your Platforms.

Activity 14

Book Platform Mapping

Get a clean piece of paper. In the center, draw a small book— that represents yours.

Your Book Title

From that center point, draw a straight line from the center to any edge of the paper. I have nine questions that will be used to complete your map.

These questions include:

What is the topic of your book?

What is your experience/expertise?

Why do you write about this?

How are you different from others in this area?

What success stories do you have on this topic or that you've experienced?

What failure stories do you have on this topic or that you've experienced?

What is the #1 thing that makes your book worthwhile?

Who is the person who desperately seeks/needs to read your book?

What two things will the reader learn?

When I created the Platform for the concept of women undermining women—one that eventually led me to concentrate on the female dominated workplace of health care—it evolved around a common phrase: conflict resolution. The following is part of the process that ties into the above questions.

1. *What is the topic of your book?*

   Along the line, write down the MAIN TOPIC of your book. Mine was conflict resolution.

Now, create branches—representing sub-topics that can relate or spin-off from it. With conflict resolution, sub-topics could include *workplace, gender, cultural, generational, health care.*

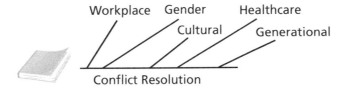

From this first set of sub-topics, are there any new topics that are connected? In my example, workplaces could have *female dominated, male dominated or integrated.*

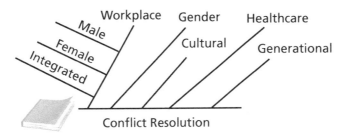

From that, I could develop additional sub-headings, as I drilled down.

2. *What is your experience/expertise?*
   Start a new main line from the book, this time, label it *experience/expertise*.

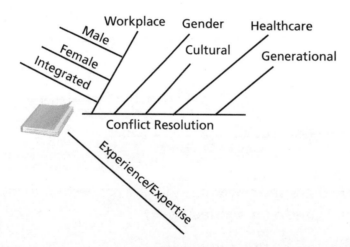

In other words, what brought me to the party ... just why was I the expert, the go-to person for this topic? With that thought, I could draw lines from the main experience/expertise line for sub-headings, identifying all the areas that my expertise came from—it could include *studies, other publications, already developed talks, media appearances, businesses*—anything that enhances my credibility and reputation.

Judith's Game Plan Design Board for "Stabotage!"

Chapter 5

Gossip, Backstabbing & Friendship

Quote: JB on gossip

Loose Tongues

Comment, stories

Gossiping

Dr. Scott LeBuke interview

Carole Hyatt interview

Nurse June Interview

Define

Self mag stats

Inside Saboteur

Comment

Edward Smolak interview

Inside Saboteur

Comment

Nurse Brenda interview

Building Positive Relationships

Susan-dental interview

Nurse Annabelle interview

MD Naomi interview

MD Georgia interview

Secty Anne interview

Nurse Sup MaryAnn interview

Clerk Sharon interview

Building Respect

MD Martha interview

MD Angela interview

Players

Pit Bulls
Skunks
Snakes
Scorpions
Slugs

descriptions, behaviors-how to deal w/

JB Keepers:
2 Tongue weighs;
Momisms

Summing Up

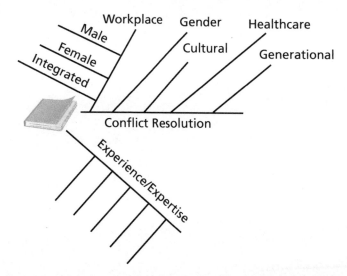

I then continued the process as I moved around my book center, creating a wheel of spokes with the remaining questions:

3. *Why do you write about this?*
4. *How are you different from others in this area?*
5. *What success stories do you have on this topic or that you've experienced?*
6. *What failure stories do you have on this topic or that you've experienced?*
7. *What is the #1 thing that makes your book worthwhile?*
8. *Who is the person who desperately seeks/needs to read your book?*
9. *What 2 things will the reader learn?*

By the time I completed the Book Mapping process, I had an amazing document in my hands. It can serve as the basis of my Platform, Plan and Pitch to others. My Platform was launched, a Platform that created over $4,000,000 in cumulative speaking engagements, books sales, consulting and corporate sponsorships over a 30-year period. A career that supported my family and built a business.

And here's your bonus—the same mapping process can be used for speech mapping based on your Book.

It's Your Turn ...

Duplicate the format of the Map for You, for your Book, your social media strategies, even your publicity plans. Keeping those nine questions in front of you will maintain your focus, providing the clarity and confidence to support your Book. You can use it to build on the various Steps of your Platforms with the main branch being one of the Steps and the sub-branches components of each.

When you truly understand the depth of what it will reveal, you buy into why you are "the one" to address the topic and create the Book— Your Book! You'll discover that not only do you have a treasure map in your hands ... you can indeed find a pot of gold.

Book Mapping for_____

What is the topic of your book?

What is your experience/expertise?

Why do you write about this?

How are you different from others in this area?

What success stories do you have on this topic or that you've experienced?

What failure stories do you have on this topic or that you've experienced?

What is the #1 thing that makes your book worthwhile?

Who is the person who desperately seeks/needs to read your book?

What two things will the reader learn?

As an Author, if you don't speak up, your silence says it's OK ... whatever "it" is.

As an author, you are now the expert—if in fiction; your characters behave in certain ways, some quite naughty—is your voice in there somewhere that gets a consequence if that bad behavior is not good? What about nonfiction? Your expertise now has a global platform capability ... are you speaking up for, or against, things that your Fans and Followers would support and cheer for you?

Or, do you keep it to yourself? We authors have quite a responsibility to do shout-outs and call-outs. Do you?

8

The Publishing Siren and Your Muse

Inspiration Keeps You From Getting Stuck

"What is The Subconscious to every other man, in its
creative aspect becomes, for writers, The Muse."

Ray Bradbury

Having a book, with your name as the author on it, adds a significant notch in the credibility game "belt." It goes beyond just a business card; it becomes part of your guts and soul. There isn't a gathering of people where someone, in fact, many ones, will share that they feel that they have a book in them.

How you came to the publishing path is often a mystery. You heard the Publishing Siren: *Come to me; here am I ... your own little island*. And you are there!

Some know from early-on that writing is in their DNA. Mega best-selling author Stephen King was like that. His books may not be your pleasure reading genre, but his gift of writing is transparent in everything he does. His nonfiction book, *On Writing*, is a personal favorite of mine and is recommended to all authors, no matter where they are on their writing journey.

There isn't a time somewhere along the path that detours and potholes don't show up. Writer's block. Or it could be a "marketing" block; "Internet use" block; even an "I'm sick of it all" block. Or, Platform Building Block. The questions become:

Authors and Muses go hand in hand.

- What will get you back on track?
- What inspires you to move forward?
- What gets your creative juices going?

Mega best-selling author Janet Evanovich has a salty sense of humor that spills out of her heroine Stephanie Plum's mouth. When Evanovich gets stuck, one of her favorite "pick me up and get me back on track" antidotes is a bag of Cheetos. Her creative juices start flowing, not to mention the glowing orange color on her keyboard!

Your Muse becomes your ally—a friend who is there in a time of need; an encourager; sometimes even a form of reward.

Activity 15

What Muse Is Yours?

Using the questions above as a springboard, identify what are the "things" you have done in the past that have been a "fall back" scenario when you've been stuck:

_____

_____

_____

_____

Creating and building Platforms requires creativity and endurance.

Knowing what works and doesn't work makes your work so much easier.

The Publishing Siren still beckons— the Muse will assist you in answering the call.

_____

_____

_____

If you could be doing anything right now that makes you laugh, what would it be?

_____

_____

_____

What music calms and soothes your soul? Who is the artist?

_____

_____

_____

Is there a movie, an author, a book or an artist that inspires you or just allows you to think or view things with a twist or different perspective? Name them and if there is a passage, scene or work that is the genesis—what is it?

_____

_____

_____

_____

Is there an environment that just fits you like a glove ... that if you had your druthers, you would be there tomorrow?

_____

_____

_____

If you had a magic wand, is there a place, sound, people, food or activity that you would embrace in a nanosecond as "yours"? What are they?

_____

_____

_____

_____

What would be your reward(s) for completing a job? Think big and small.

_____

_____

_____

_____

Do some mixing and matching. For me, the magic wand always delivers water and sun. Always. I live in the Rocky Mountains, but at heart, I'm the girl who grew up on the beach. My idea of something fabulous is warm sand under my feet; snorkeling; getting a few rays of sun. Being on a cruise is like a delicious chocolate to me. Slipping into the hot tub with a cup of tea is a perfect way to start or end a day.

I don't have the gift of creating or playing music, but I have the gift to enjoy it. A fabulous piano concerto is perfect for background; Rachmaninoff's *Theme from Paganini* is at the top of my favorites' list, with one movement in it that thrills me and allows my thoughts to soar when I lean back in a chair and close my eyes.

Foreign languages are my tongue's stumbling block. I don't understand Italian, but I can sense the passion in the words of an opera—something that I love to have on in the background when I edit.

Rewards come in all kinds of shapes and sizes. One of my favorites is reading what I call trashy novels—mystery and action thrillers. The other is taking a cruise or finding a beach to plunk down on. When I finish writing a book, I get to read one just for fun—always. What's amazing is that when I let my mind go in a totally different direction from what my normal range of writing is, I get ideas—ideas that I can use in my own writing that have been generated from an unconnected genre. The Muse is present … The cost of my rewards can range from just a few dollars to a thousand plus.

Water is throughout my home and office—water features on the front porch; in several rooms; during the spring and fall months, there are two outdoor ponds that I see and hear; I move my writing office to a tree-enclosed space where I can see and hear water and nature—water is my Muse.

Just knowing that I can tap into some form of what my triggers are enables me to engage a blockbuster when needed. Find yours, no matter how trivial it or they seem.

Authoring is like a roller coaster … sometimes you are up; sometimes you are down; but you've got to stay in the seat.

Life happens for authors. Sometimes it's smooth, others—total chaos. Some weeks, all the magic words drop in and others, you feel that you've been depleted. It happens. Knowing what your muse is—what inspires you and kick-starts or gets you back on track is essential. Having your "people" in your circle that you can reach out to is critical. And not having people in your circle who are nay-sayers and distract you from your Book Vision is vital for your survival in the writing and publishing process.

Listening to your favorite music to tap into may open up your creative channels. Or even watching your favorite movie that makes you laugh until you are almost incontinent may do the trick.

It's a roller coaster out here. Authoring is never a flat ride … and think how boring it would be if it was! Find your muse and add it to your Village.

9

The Time Factor

De-Clutter and Prioritize Now

"Writing is easy. All you do is stare at a blank sheet of paper until drops of blood form on your forehead."

Gene Fowler

There are a number of things that can roadblock authors and get them into trouble with their Platforms. At the top of the list is the Time Factor—not finding it ... not committing to it ... or not taking it.

Most authors have great intentions. They have an idea they feel Passionate about; they work on fine-tuning their Vision; and they even make a Commitment to support their Book. Yet something burps up and gets in the way. There's always one more thing that needs to be done, or so they think. They won't put their pencils down, wanting to tweak their draft one more time or do one more interview or revamp a character one more time or ... fill in the blank.

It just doesn't get done. Whatever the one more thing is—it prevents them from reaching and crossing the finishing line with completed book in hand. It's similar to the old adage, one for the money, two for the show, three to get ready ... and then "stuck" happens at three to get ready ... three to get ready ... they never go! And they never get their book.

Sound familiar? So many wannabe authors have the Passion; they talk about their forthcoming book; they even have a Vision for what they want it to be; yet they fail to Commit to creating the time to create and complete their book. You can never get to "four to GO" unless you make the time. To write your book. To develop your Platforms. Time ... your friend, and your enemy.

Activity 16

How Do You Spend Your Day, Your Time?

How do you spend your time? The following Activity is designed to look closely at how you spend yours.

1. **List all your daily activities carefully, and then group them.**
   Allocate a percentage of your daily time to each grouping with a brief explanation about the activity.

   _____   _____

   _____   _____

   _____   _____

   _____   _____

   _____   _____

   _____   _____

   _____   _____

   _____   _____

2. Draw a circle for each group. The number of circles you will have will be dependent on the number of groupings.

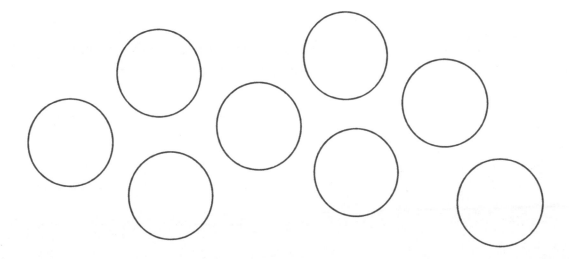

For example, if you spend 40 percent of your day working, label a circle "Work" with its percentage. If you decide that Exercising and Eating are within the same group totaling 10 percent, label a circle "Eating and Exercise" and it's percentage. If you spend 30 percent of your day sleeping, label a circle "Sleep" with its percentage. If you spend 10 percent dedicated to family time, section it off and label it "Family." If you spend 10 percent of your day on education, label it "Education." Etc. Do this with all your groupings.

3. Complete your circles with your groups and percentages. Your percentages should total 100.

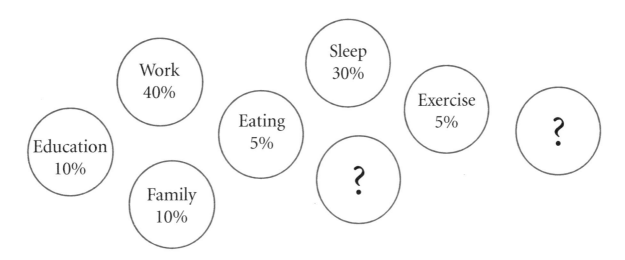

Any surprises? What percentage did you allocate to your Authoring and to your Book? How are you spending your *Time*? You've got a book to write; to finish; and to market. It's all part of the total Platform. This is the time to look inside with realism and truth, as you address your project.

Do you have the Time?

Can you make the Time?

Will you make the Time?

Your goal is to allocate your entire day so that you know where your time goes. When you Commit to your Author and Book Platforms, usually something is going to have to "go." Where are you going to find your time to complete your Vision and tap into your Passion?

Finding your authoring time can be a challenge. There will be detours and a few roadblocks along the way. Some will come from the obvious: work consumes a lot of your time; so does sleeping—most likely a minimum of 70 percent of your day is consumed by those two activities. The rest will be split among a variety of personal and professionally related items including you.

Remember what was said earlier ... I'm going to repeat those statements again and again throughout this Guidebook as you hone in on developing your Platforms.

This is the time you need to become myopic. If your goal is to create your book; to launch it; and be successful—however you define success—focus is your new middle name.

If you have a family, call a Family Powwow. Talk about your book; let them know that it's not just a few hours or a weekend project ... It's going to take many months. You want to give them a heads up—a vacation of choice that includes you happens after the book is completed; that you need specific time to get into your writing zone ... and when you are there, there is a "no entrance allowed" sign outside of your writing space; that you need a "zone" around you that allows you total freedom to sometimes just stare off into space as you gather your thoughts. It's important to let them know that daily tasks as simple as prepping breakfast or being the family taxi driver need to be reassigned.

As the Book Shepherd, I become the author's advocate, sometimes communicating to those family members what the needs are for the author during this time and reminding the author of his needs.

It's important for you to address the self-sabotage issue if it is lurking. You wouldn't be doing your book unless you believed in it. But, and it's a big BUT, it's incredibly easy to get waylaid in the process—done at your own hands.

Where Are You Hanging Your Authoring Hat?

Your space is important. Some authors are happy as clams writing their books in busy coffee shops; others have special rooms or places they have to go.

A place like Starbucks would be the last place to find me—you would have better luck finding me around water—on a cruise ship; a backyard deck with the sound of the ocean, stream, river or pond in the background—water is my muse. What's important is to find yours—find what puts your authoring genius in play.

Sometimes your space will be dictated by what doesn't work for you. You may have a perfectly good "quiet" office in your home, but it's loaded with distractions. Little ones may cry; family members can pop in and out; both family and friends sometimes get confused with someone who "works" out of the home … and writing is work. They think that if you are physically there, that you really aren't "working."

My first book was carved out in my offices. Two afternoons were set aside each week to exclusively work on it with a writing coach. My staff was told, "No calls or interruptions unless it was urgent—like John or the kids were in an accident." I didn't know that I was more productive around water … that awareness evolved. What I did know was that I had to have uninterrupted time and that it wouldn't work at home—three teenagers and a gaggle of pets that kids often have, and being chief cook in the evening were my primary distractions.

If your home is comparable to Grand Central Station, writing will be difficult at best. Find your spot; claim it; and shut the door.

What's important is to find out how best you write and set up a protocol that will allow you to be at peak authoring performance.

Think back ... where have you been in a peak performance time in your career ... in your life? What brought you there? How did it feel?

These are the clues that will lead to your authoring success.

How Do You Write?

Your methodology of writing is important. I don't do well in the piece-meal writing world; an hour here and an hour there. I'm a binge writer—creating huge blocks within a short period of time. If you and I were talking, I might say, "Today, I will write two chapters." And do it. The entire audio program was created over two days that *Author YOU: Creating and Building Your Author and Book Platform* was designed for. Now, that doesn't count my years of publishing that led up to it, but the binge factor was in play.

"Carrots" are important. Rewards should be treats—which could be scheduling a massage, an hour or two to dive into a missed episode of a favorite show that has been TIVOed, even a soak in a bubble bath.

For me, there is always hot tea close by or my favorite peach ice tea. When the first draft of a chapter is completed, I get a reward. With my *Stabotage!* book, it was a handful of M&Ms every time a chapter was completed; for another, an escape to a favorite movie. When the book is finished, I get my ultimate reward—a full month of reading trashy novels (suspense thrillers are my choice).

De-Cluttering Your Life and Creating Time

Have you ever heard, or felt, a giant sucking sound? Do you feel the whirling forces pulling you into old places where life is hectic, full of distractions, pressures and jealousies? Its battle cry keeps you focused on the unimportant. The *time* gremlin—your enemy.

What lurks behind that friendly handshake and beguiling smile; that pleasant phone call; or those countless emails and Facebook requests, Twitter follows or Repinning? Deception—almost invisible—stumbling blocks linger. Intentionally or not, they trip you up and throw you out of the publishing dance. These are friends, co-workers and others who ask small favors—a few minutes here, a few minutes there.

Initially, they appear harmless, but collectively, they have a huge effect on the quality of your writing and Platform building.

If completing your book is important to you, then it belongs at the top—or near the top—of your personal priority list.

If building your crowd—those people who will support you and for whom your book is a priority—it moves up to the top of your list. If finding more time to build on the Commitment phase of the Platform is critical, something has got to give—finding

Good authors and writers know that they must delegate and discard.

Delegate the things that need to be done but you don't enjoy; and discard anything that is a distraction or no longer relevant.

In other words, it's time to eliminate your clutter.

Clutter doesn't necessarily mean "stuff."—it can be anything that can get you off track.

the time to support your Vision has become a priority. The common problem encountered with so many authors is that they are pulled in every direction: Work, family, school, self, commitments and the biggest one ... excuses.

Activity 17

What's Your Priority?

Quick ... identify the top four things in your life—personal or work-related. Write them down—just a few words. Do it quickly.

1. _____

2. _____

3. _____

4. _____

Of the four, draw a line through the one that is least important. Work backwards. Draw a line through the next least important until you get to the last remaining item.

My question for you becomes: Do you spend the amount of time you want on the remaining item on your list—the one that has become "number one"?

If you are like my typical author clients and audiences I speak to, most likely you don't. Clutter—distraction— is the primary culprit—invading your life at every crack and crevice.

It's reassessment time—if you continue to allow large chunks of your time to be placed into areas that are really not important, not critical, the odds are that your book will be put on the back shelf, delayed, or come out disjointed. And, there's a possibility that it just might never happen.

One more time:

> *If you never say "no," your "yeses" become worthless.*
> *Don't do well what you have no business doing.*

As an author, you need to prioritize.
It's that simple. And that complicated.

De-Cluttering Paves Your Way

If you feel you are surrounded by chaos, most likely you are. If you feel that your life has become a giant octopus, pulling you in eight different ways, it most likely has. There isn't an author who hasn't had to clear out some of the clutter to unclog his or her space.

When I ready myself for the writing of a new book, there's a ritual I go through to de-clutter and prep. There's a cleaning/clearing frenzy that everything that is not needed is moved out of sight in my office. The expandable files with information I've been storing are invited into view and spread out for the project, sometimes on the rug—not to be put away until I'm finished.

No one is allowed into my inner office when "stuff" is out. Imagine a "do not cross" yellow tape—the one you see on TV in *NCIS* or *Castle*—across its French doors. Staff doesn't come in; hubby can't come in; grandkids can't come in; cleaning person is not allowed in. No one is allowed in or out ... only me. When I'm done, it all goes back to a box or file and the tape comes off. It's my authoring space and only available to others by invitation.

What creates a giant sucking sound … a sound that takes your time and energy that results in non-completion? How about:

- *organizations that take your time, and you really care little about;*
- *your job that's not a joy to be at;*
- *your job that has huge demands on you;*
- *lack of money;*
- *fear of using money for your book project;*
- *relationships;*
- *fear of writing;*
- *not knowing how to organize a book;*
- *fear of being vulnerable;*
- *your own lack of confidence;*
- *your failure to give yourself permission;*
- *lack of organizational skills—be it time, files or routines;*
- *TV or video games;*
- *others not believing in you, your idea or ability to write it;*
- *being leery of technology—or just goofing off.*

And that's just a starting list. As an author, it is easy to get pulled away from your vision. Others do it, and you do it.

Activity 18
Name Your Cluttering Gremlins

I've identified several—it's time for you to ID yours.

_____

_____

_____

_____

_____

_____

_____

_____

_____

Activity 19

Identifying Your Stuff And What You Really…

…Need to Get to Pull Your Platform Together

Every author has stuff—stuff that is critical to complete writing the book; some stuff that is needed to support the writing every once in awhile; and stuff that is just stuff—stuff that can begin to sound like "noise." Ditto for Platform building. Think connecting with others; joining "like" groups; allocating moneys; building a team, etc. What's yours?

_____   _____

_____   _____

_____   _____

_____   _____

_____   _____

_____   _____

_____   _____

_____   _____

Now, write down everything that is in your work area. Include everything you think you need to reach success in your Platform building.

_____

_____

_____

_____

_____

_____

_____

Is it crucial for this stage? If it is not—label it "C."

C

If it is something that you will most likely need to use sometime during the Platform building, label it a "B."

B

If it is something that you will be getting your hands on daily, it belongs in your "A" pile.

A

Rearrange your lists—whether you do it in columns that you can see on a white board, flip chart, a posted sheet of paper or something you see first thing when you open your computer doesn't matter. What matters is that you "visit" it daily to keep you FOCUSED ... and de-cluttered.

At the top will be everything that is an "A"—things that you use often and do not make sense to remove from your site. Items such as your computer; your Post-its; any writing software or programs; a flash drive (always, always have a separate backup of your daily work—even when you have an offsite source—you never know when you may be away from your primary writing site and inspirations strike); and reference books and specific files that relate to the current project you are working on. Don't forget to include your refreshments—from a favorite beverage, to a snack, to a reward.

In "B," which supplies that you don't need daily—reams of paper, ink for your printer, other books that you "might" need to refer to, filing cabinet for re-lated materials. If you write with background music, an inventory of CDs or a comfortable chair to shift to for a change. Maybe a pillow for your lower back.

A "C" will be items that are occasional. Any moneys spent on your project need to be tracked—a receipt envelop or file that will be used for accounting; things that are "to do" ... to do when?

If you are highly visual like I am, you probably need to see all your stuff. I can't totally file anything away out of sight until I'm done with it. Why? Because depending on how creative I feel when I get the urge to file, is where the item will land. What I put away on a Tuesday may not be where my creative brain is on a Saturday. My solution is to have a "C" box/basket on the floor—it all gets moved off the desk, out of sight in a corner. I know it's there, just not cluttering my visual work area. Out of temporary sight, but easily retrievable when I'm done or at least know where to find it if I need it.

Some of what I'm proposing may seem silly—but trust me. I've worked with thousands of authors—all have patterns, habits and hiccups that clutter their time and processes. Find yours—you'll discover that Time you didn't know was there surfaces. Time that can be used to add to your Platform building infrastructure.

JB's
Keeper 9

If you never say *NO*,
your *YESES* are worthless.

Oh boy … how many times have you said "yes" to something, then wanted to kick yourself in the tush for doing so? It's not uncommon to say "yes" to get someone out of your hair—after all, you are putting so much energy into resisting him or her in the first place. Mom always said that if you want something done—give it to a busy person.

Get Mom out of your head. You need to say "no"—clear, concise and direct. When you are in the *authoring* way, you don't need more on your plate. Better for those around you to be savvy and astute—and take the pressure off you. The goal is to finish the book—not chair the committee, at least this year.

10

Social Media Creates Your Marketing Platform

It's a New, New Connected World

"How can you squander even one more day not taking
advantage of the greatest shifts of our generation?
How dare you settle for less when the world has
made it so easy for you to be remarkable?"

Seth Godin

If you are resistant to social media—whether *Twitter, Facebook, LinkedIn, YouTube, Blogs, Google+, Pinterest* or whatever else comes along, get over it. They are a fact of marketing You and your Book. Where you can't leave home without your Platforms; you can't leave home without knowing something about social media and its power.

Getting started can be a challenge, especially when you don't think you have the time, and in some cases, the patience. As with anything new, the key word here is learning. And as adult learners, you try to fit all of this new information into an often out-of-date view of the world. So, not only are you learning a new skill, you have no reference point for its meaning. Adult learners like reference points. Sometimes, the more, the better.

Social Media Is a Trend, Not a Fad

Finding the time becomes almost as overwhelming as grasping all the new ideas and concepts that are whirling within the social media world. Warp speed becomes the operative methodology. Getting started, searching for steps that made sense in implementing a social media strategy seems like an impossible feat.

You can succeed in this arena by taking it a step at a time. You are not re-inventing new content to send out; it's all within the pages of your book. And there is you—the brains behind it, the expert, the story teller. Every chapter has morsels that can be shared in bytes and bites. The Internet delivers your presence to potentially millions of fans and followers. Someone who finds your words, chews on them and discovers that they are the perfect appetizer, main course or dessert. Welcome to the 21st Century.

Activity 20

What Social Media Tools Are You Using?

Quick ... mark all the different social media tools you currently have/use:

___ Facebook

___ Twitter

___ LinkedIn

___ YouTube channel

___ Google+

___ Blog

___ Hootsuite

___ SocialOomph

___ WordPress

___ iStockPhoto

___ Squidoo

___ Slideshare

___ PowerPoint

___ Mobile Marketing

___ Pinterest

___ Tweetdeck

___ Tubemogul

___ Ping.fm

___ Tumblr

___ Ning

___ TweetDeck

___ Animoto

___ Blogger

___ Flickr

___ Google Analytics

___ FeedShark

___ DreamsTime

___ Buzzstream

___ QR code

___ Other (ID or name)

Creating Your Social Media Presence

Most likely, you didn't mark them all ... it doesn't matter ... at least, yet. With your Book Platform, it's critical to begin mastering the social media crowd. It's huge; it's growing; and it can make your book. Begin with:

Stage One: Revisit your Vision

For most authors, this includes having their voice heard, their story told and having a group of loyal fans and, of course, book sales. Is there any buzz starting about You and your Book? Have you directed anyone to buy it on Amazon? Are you asking EVERYBODY to post positive, 5-Star "your book rocks" reviews? *Do not, do not, do not be shy here.* Other buyers read those reviews. Amazon asks, "Was this review helpful" on each book's page. They make a difference—the more you get, the better for your Book.

Stage Two: Focus on Content and Connect

This Step has two critical components that are somewhat interchangeable—content can be designed based on the trends and hot topics on the Internet.   Search for what people are talking about and connect with them. Follow their blogs, make comments, and reach out.

   When you are ready to do a full book launch, these blogs, especially those within your field and topic of expertise, become the perfect partner. You may be invited to guest blog; they may write a review of your book and post it within their blog ... your words and information about your book goes viral. It's a very good thing! You may never "meet" a blog partner, but they have the ability to become the "good neighbor"—like the one that you can count on that lives next door or across the street that will be there when you need them.

Google SEARCH, Twitter Search, and *Alexia.com* are the key Internet tools to use. Here you will find what the hot topics are, find related links, competition and ideas for your content. You will discover how many times a word or phrase is used on a monthly basis when someone—anyone—places within a search engine's "search" function.

For content, start with your book, articles and blog. You will have difficulty moving to the more intermediate stage of publishing until you have content and can address that content toward the conversation that is occurring on the Internet.

Social media is about staying in the moment, staying current, and looking for trends. Part of the point of social media is to make your followers look good, stay connected and provide valuable content. Seventy percent of the content you deliver needs to be helpful, informative and perhaps sassy and salty—an idea or concept that will make the reader sit up and take notice. Another 20 percent is sharing information about your book and 5 to 10 percent is being a bit personal.

Being authentic is a key element in your social media strategy.

Stage 3: Managing Your Time with Smarts

Social media can be a time vampire. You, the savvy author, must manage it—a task, especially in the early stages as being overwhelming.

Initially, you don't know what you are doing, you just have a feeling you want to do it or were told that you need to do it—because everyone else is doing it. But, it seems that for most, they aren't necessarily managing it—it is managing them. You feel lost, and desperately want to be found. Balance is essential here, yet wobbly has become your middle name.

To master it, you need a management platform that works for you. Below is a list of many of the programs that can help you to move through this stage.

- *Ping.fm*: Created for the sole purpose of making it as easy as possible to share your posts with the world, *Ping.fm* fills the bill. Now you don't have to fumble around the web in order to post anymore, you can just post once, and be done with it.

  Whenever you put a post, a Tweet, or a photo in one location, such as *Flickr* or *Facebook*, *Ping.fm* sends it to all the other social media sites and social media syndication sites—automatically. This allows you to make the most of your time and effort. Your content is now reaching a much bigger audience.

  Ping.fm is about content syndication. Among other things, it manages *Flickr*, the photo-sharing site. If you post photos on *Flickr*, they will automatically be sent to all your other communities. It also will help you manage *Delicious, NIG, GoogleBuzz*, and 30 other tools, including *PR Newswire*.

- *Hootsuite:* With *Hootsuite*, you can monitor keywords, manage multiple *Twitter, Facebook, LinkedIn, Google+, Ping.fm* and *WordPress* profiles, schedule messages, coordinate multiple contributors, assign tasks, monitor mentions, retweets and spread messages over multiple platforms. Ideal for setting up a week, even a month of information that will be funneled out over a period of time at specific hours.

Going on vacation, but don't want to disappear from cyberspace? *Hootsuite* becomes your best friend. A basic account on *HootSuite* is free, so get on there and check out what it can do for you! The free account is very good. There is also a Pro version, when you're ready to upgrade to a higher level of management including additional accounts to post for as well as users. It's one of my favorite tools.

- *TweetDeck.com* has functions that are very similar to *HootSuite*, but they each have a totally different look and feel.

  TweetDeck IDs itself as "your personal browser for staying in touch with what's happening now, connecting you with your contacts across *Twitter, Facebook, LinkedIn* and more."

  With *TweetDeck*, anyone can tweet like a pro. See what people are saying about you and join the conversation by tweeting, sharing photos, videos or links directly from *TweetDeck*. This tool is the ideal choice when you have a huge Twitter community, or you anticipate building one.

- *SocialOopmh.com* is a free tool for managing a social media program and allows you to automatically follow people who follow you if you choose to do so. This saves you a lot of time and your "Friends list" builds itself. There are pros and cons to auto-following. Pick the strategy that works for you.

  Every time someone new follows you, *SocialOomph* automatically sends them a customizable thank you note from you. You don't even have to think about it once you set it up.

Don't try to sell them anything in the thank you note. Let them know the kind of content you're going to be giving them on an ongoing basis, maybe give them a link to your website, suggest that you have regular postings on the *Facebook* Fan page for following and say thanks. That's it.

SocialOomph also lets you schedule posts and Tweets. It has many more unique features, so take a look at this excellent free tool. They also have a Pro version.

GoogleAlerts and *SocialOomph* have similarities. At the end of the day, each sends a recap of anyone who has used your name in a Tweet, @reply, sent a direct message to you or retweeted one of your postings. It's a good feature to have to let you know who is talking about you.

- *Tumblr:* Is there anything this site doesn't do? From blogs … did you know with this site you can call in your blog post and it will be sent out to multiple sites like *Facebook* and *Twitter*? The "photosets" link suggests that it is part of the future of books.

- *Ning:* Besides being a tool for building a community platform, it has the ability to carry your unique "look." Initially, it started out as a free tool for any and all but converted to a paid platform in 2010. What's distinctive about *Ning* is that it has similarities to *Facebook*, but has the ability to customize what you want to look like on the Internet without the template restriction that a Facebook delivers (along with the ever-changing "look" that *Facebook* frequently does). I'm not saying to not do *Facebook*—this is a must platform to play in. But with *Ning*, depending on your topic and expertise, you can really create a "go-to" spot. It's ideal for niche marketing.

- *YouTube:* If TV is for viewing, entertainment and learning, *YouTube* is an excellent resource. Owned by *Google*, you can post presentations, videos of your events, share the powerful videos you will make on one of my favorites, *Animoto*. Getting a discussion going keeps people connected, which is what the Internet and social media is all about.

  As an author, one of the first things you should do is create a *YouTube* channel—post to it regularly with new videos—usually best to limit them to a few minutes. You then let others know what's happening—include links to them within your *Twitter, Facebook, Google+, LinkedIn, Pinterest* and *Blog* postings.

  Believe it or not, *YouTube* is now the #1 channel watched today. Get You and your Book up there.

- *TubeMogul.com* is all about syndicating video. If you upload a video onto *YouTube*, you're only inside the *YouTube* community. If you upload it to *TubeMogul* instead, it is distributed to multiple platforms that house video information, like *Blip TV, YouTube, Edge Cast,* and the other big video distribution websites. It also crunches analytics and gives you feedback about your video efforts including how long someone watches one of your videos and how many times it has viewed.

  TubeMogul will syndicate one video to many different platforms to really make the most of the energy you put in to producing it. All for free. A good deal, for sure.

- *Facebook:* A major presence of the Internet with over one billion users, *Facebook* is a great way to deepen relationships with your remote readers. Really. They become true followers for, and of, your work. *Facebook* can send people to your blog where they can get the more in-depth information you want to share. *Facebook* has Fan pages where you can grow your community, create discussion boards, share videos of your events and keep your followers in the loop on breakthroughs, insights and factoids. If you aren't set up on *Facebook*, do it ... now's the time ... *www.Facebook.com*.

  Whenever I hear news about an *Author U* member and *Book Shepherd* client, I post it on the Author U Fan page (*www.Facebook.com/AuthorU*) along with the author's book link on *Amazon*. Same thing with Book Shepherd clients; it gets posted on its Facebook page (*www.Facebook.com/ TheBookShepherd*) with links to *Amazon, YouTube*, their blog or anything else that ties the story in with the item posted. Check out the Notes Application to put your blog up.

- *LinkedIn:* When you think *LinkedIn*—think group. Not only can you share your work experience and business interests here, you can join Groups and create one. These Groups can be topic specific and related to your book—and they are a reputation builder—the real power of *LinkedIn*. Commenting on a conversation stream not only helps your ranking in the search engines, it builds your reputation.

Better yet, create a Group around your book or topic. Invite others, add their voice, their expertise, and start a group discussion. You are the moderator. Keep it open so others can freely make comments. Some of these online communities are huge. I have them at *Author U* and *The Book Shepherd* on *LinkedIn*—join in the discussion!

- *Google+:* One of the newest kids on the block, *Google+* has created some sophisticated strategies for building communities. With its arsenal of tools and apps, it's a freebie to join. You connect with friends and like-minded people in *Circles*, can interact in real time using the *Google+* Hangout feature and create a business page.

  Google+ is not the size of *Facebook* or *Twitter*, but it's growing rapidly and still fairly young in its evolution cycle. The question always becomes: "How many of these bloody things do I have to belong to?" With something like *Hootsuite* in your tool kit, the answer is, "Many." *Google+* has sophistication about it—and with its direct link to the mother ship of search engines, *Google*; it can't be ignored or discounted. Set up a profile, start your *Circles* and just do it.

  "How many of these bloody things do I have to belong to?"

- *Twitter:* Besides *Facebook*, this revolutionary site has altered communications—all within 140 characters, including spaces and punctuation. Editing is critical … with a max of 140 characters, you learn to condense quickly. Forget about telling everyone about your breakfast menu; add more meat to your topic. You can blast out events, meetings, ahas, anything to other associated sites like *Twitter.com/search* and *NearbyTweets.com* that in turn connect tweeters locally. Using a program like *Hootsuite* mentioned above is ideal to keep it organized and efficient—and sane.

  Think of *Twitter* as a cocktail party on steroids. Information moves rapidly—tweeting once a day isn't enough; you will create "campaigns" in getting your messages out that are around your Book

Platform—all with the goal to drive the reader and first "follows" you to become a believer and a buyer. The power of *Twitter* comes when your message is consider "hot"—it is retweeted to others within your follower's *Twitter* network. Use hashtags (#) within your Tweet—it gets further outreach. All done virally and rapidly. Tweets have a lifespan of 15 seconds to an hour.

And, it has become one of the "go to" places where producers, journalists and other media professional are looking for experts. Having your blog linked with *Twitter* is a powerful tool to increase your credibility and that's why authors need to use it. It keeps you current in a way your website can not do. Putting your *Twitter* stream on the Home page of your website keeps it current at all times—and only the tweets you put out show.

- *Pinterest:* If your audience is female, get to *Pinterest* now—a visual quilt of activity. Why? Over 80 percent of *Pinterest* users are women. It is fairly simple to use—you create "boards" of interest— your interests. These boards are visual displays—photos, sayings—you name it. Add to them and share.

  When others see them, they in turn, can "repin" and share with anyone they know. *Pinterest* is currently the fastest-growing social media community.

- *Blogs:* You need one. Some are heavier in content than others. With the advent of *Twitter,* most *Blogs* have become shorter in the length of material presented. You can use your name, your book title, a key word or phrase (a must to do in titles and within the content) … you've got lots of options. Your *Blog* should be on your website with the ability for visitors to sign-up for it.

As an author, you want to visit other blogs in your topic area—make comments; you could be invited to do a guest blog. I do guest blogging often for the Tattered Cover Book Store in Colorado. Getting your name out, especially in blogland, adds to your credibility factor. *Google* tracks blogs and links to websites; the more you show up, the greater your ranking. The result: increased visibility.

- *WordPress:* The preferred platform for most *Blogs is WordPress* (*www.WordPress.com*) … you can also use *Google's Blogger or Tumblr*. There are other platforms as well, some free, some with a fee. *WordPress* has excellent support and flexibility—and it's free. Think user-friendly when you think of *WordPress*. *WordPress* is also my recommended platform for building your website on.

- *Blogger* is another blogging platform choice, owned by *Google*. Because it's so easy, you can have your *Blog* up and running within 15 minutes—so think instant. As with instant things, don't expect a huge amount of options and flexibility as *WordPress* offers, but it will do in a pinch.

- *Flickr:* How would you like to have access to millions of images? That's what *Flickr* can do for you. *Flickr* community members have granted the right to use their images on blogs, websites, newsletters and video. Before you use any image, make sure you check with the Usage Rights request of the owner of the image that what you want to use it for is okay. Also, make sure you give appropriate credit under any image that you use.

- *iStockPhoto and DreamsTime:* Both these sites add images monthly—photos, audio and video clips that can be downloaded for free. It's worthwhile to check in with them every once in awhile— if you see something that just might be a fit for a project you are thinking of, a new talk, book or your current one, grab it so you have it. Websites are *www.IStockPhoto.com* and *www.DreamsTime.com/free-photos.*

- *Squidoo:* Seth Godin, author and marketing genius of a zillion books is a fan of *Squidoo*. This simple publishing platform and community allows you to create "lenses" online. Each page is a simple website or flyer, allowing you to post articles on anything about your topic of interest. It captures your unique perspective. And, the cool thing about *Squidoo* is that you can even earn royalties for a charity of your choice.

- *FeedShark:* A great tool that promotes your blog, website, RSS feed and podcasts to the Internet. It can be found at *FeedShark.BrainBliss.com.*

- *BuzzStream:* This site is a management site with two primary functions: monitoring and source identification and link partnership performance tracking. It will track sites like *Twitter* and *Linkedin* and *blogs* and becomes within time, a database for you. Combining your various contacts that come via other Internet sources was unheard of not long ago. Not now.

Now, it's time to kick it up. Let's look at some of the other bells and whistles that you can work with and use to enhance what you are about in the development and display of your content. With these sites, syndication is the goal. You want the world to know who you are and what your book is about!

- Create articles from chapters you have written in your book. Why create something from scratch all the time, it's right at your fingertips within your computer. With articles that you've already written, or a section within your book, tweak it with a new spin and make it an article. Connect it with something in the news. Sites like *www.MyArticleNetwork.com* are not free, but can save you enormous amounts of time. It will send content to other sites that need great content for their own blogs, positioning you on multiple platforms.

- *Unique Article Wizard* is a similar site. It works to drive traffic to your website and could be thought of as advertising and part of your marketing budget. *www.UniqueArticleWizard.com.*

- Take some of that content and make a PowerPoint presentation and load it on to *SlideShare, www.SlideShare.com. Slideshare* connects to *Twitter, LinkedIn, Google+* and *Facebook.* The result is that your program that you created with some type of graphics/visuals is now sent out to many platforms and search engines.

- One of my personal favorites is *Animoto*, a tool I introduce to all the authors I work with. At *www.Animoto.com*, you will discover a whole new world at your fingertips. There's a free 30-second version and one that you can create for much longer. Pop for the extra $30 a year, and create multiple videos with the use of slides that you create directly onsite. Add a little music and some "flash" and Hollywood will begin to flow through your veins.
What can you make? Why, a trailer, a form of video, a commercial—anything about you and your book. You download photos, graphics, create works and short phrases and with the *Animoto* magic

click, an amazing array of clips are merged together to create a customized video by you, now the producer. And yes, they even give you a library of free music to download to add to the experience.

This little magic maker is perfect for creating a low-low-low budget book trailer in a matter of moments. You can even load other videos and music and, along with your photos and text, you create your own high quality, well-produced video. Either way, this is a perfect tool for welcoming fans to your website, fan page and *LinkedIn* sites. Check out what I did on the *Author U* Home page at *www.AuthorU.org*.

- *TubeMogul* is one of the best tools to get your video out on multiple platforms. It is a free service that provides a single point for deploying videos to the top video and social networking sites and helps you with that syndication goal. *TubeMogul* also provides analytics, which enables you to see who is watching.

- *QR Codes* have become common in any type of branding or marketing campaign. Each *QR code* is unique in the date and links it carries, although they all look "alike." A series of lines, dots, squiggles in a small box specially IDs you, your book, your website, whatever you want. To access it, the user needs a smart phone and its wi-fi immediately links him or her to your message.

What's Next?

Social media morphs daily. A crystal ball couldn't keep up with all the products, changes and disappearances that are now common place. What's hot this week will have a new generation, the next. It means you have to pay attention; stay current; and be aware that new tools will be available to you.

Expect to see gigantic bursts of marketing creativity through Mobile Marketing as it begins building its presence. If your book is designed for the under 40, you must have Mobile Marketing in your game plan. If your readers have a smart phone, Mobile Marketing is in your immediate future.

Whatever social media additions come along, they will promise amazing opportunities for You and your Book. The key is not to wait. Use the tools available now. The next, next generation will only add to your abundance.

Don't do well what you have no business doing.

Famous last words for we authors ... it's so easy to get caught up in "things"—things that our friends think we might like to do, or should; things that can gobble up unbelievable amounts of time—be it charity, volunteering to host your organization's big event, even dog-sitting your best friend's pooch. This isn't the time.

When you are deep into your book, myopic becomes the operative word. You have to be ... otherwise you may end up ATNB ... all talk, no book.

If you aren't a walking, talking geek, there are many out there who are. And a kid in high school or college may just be the perfect person to "get" your book and become your right hand in developing a social media strategy for a minimal amount of money.

11

Internet Checklist for People Platform Building

Who's Who in the Author's Cyberworld

"The Internet is becoming the town square
for the global village of tomorrow."
Bill Gates

Love it or hate it, the Internet is and will be a key player in building your Platforms and marketing yourself and your book. If there is a resistance factor, get over it now. Either start the submersion yourself or hire someone who can help you. There are plenty of savvy, techno-savvy individuals who live and breathe the stuff. They will become your allies at this important and critical junction. This is where your People part of the Platform can rapidly accelerate.

Activity 21

How Internet Savvy Are You?

How Internet Marketing Savvy are you ... really? For each box checked, give yourself 1 point; for the boxes which ask how many times you have done an activity, you get 1 point plus a bonus point each time the activity was performed.

Phase One

- Internet Marketing Goals Defined
  - Desired Sales
  - Tribe/Readers/Fans identified
  - Goal to be leader of the Tribe (Bonus 3 points)
- Website Strategy created—including color schemes, graphics, content
- Keywords and phrases identified that will be used in all content
- Domain name registered

- Domain names of useful misspellings or names close to yours purchased
- Domain names of misspellings or names close to yours that are directed to your Home page
- WordPress Hosting
- Author picture and bio completed and loaded
- Video completed and loaded
- Copy of book cover on home page of website created
- Contact Information easily found on Home page
- Testimonials on website
- Ongoing movement on Home page (such as Facebook or Twitter postings)

Phase Two

- Facebook page established
- Author Facebook page
  - Pictures (bonus point)
  - Video (bonus point)
- Book Title Facebook page
  - Pictures (bonus point)
  - Video (bonus point)
- Facebook Fan page
  - Comments made by others on your page (bonus point)

- Twitter Account created
  - Number of Tweets per week
  - Number of re-tweets of your Tweet (bonus point)
  - The number of hashtags (#) identified that you use
- Pinterest Account created
  - Boards uploaded
  - Photos uploaded
- Blog created
- Number of Followers (yes, you get a point per follower)
- Number of people you follow (same as above)
- LinkedIn Account created (a must for business books)
- Number of LinkedIn Recommendations Received
- Number of LinkedIn Groups you have joined
- Number of LinkedIn Groups you created and moderate
- Google+ Account created
- SlideShare loaded
- Animoto Account
- YouTube Account
- Your video on YouTube (3 Bonus Points)
- Flipcam videos posted anywhere (3 Bonus Points)

Phase Three

- Ping.fm
- Tumblr
- Tube Mogul
- Google Trends
- Good Analytics
- Hootsuite
- SocialOomph
- Know number of site visits per week
- Quarterly Push
- Daily Tweets
- QR Code
- Number of Blogs per week
- Number of comments made on leading Blogs
- Number of articles posted
  - *www.UniqueArticleWizard.com*
  - *www.MyArticleNetwork.com*
  - *www.Wordpreneur.com*
  - *www.eZineArticles.com*

Score:

---

0 – 40	Oops, wake-up! You need to talk to The Book Shepherd about social media time management, a creative kick start and/or a referral to assist you in implementing a strategy that will synch with you and your book pronto.
40 – 100	You are on your way, intensify your efforts for the next two weeks and watch miracles begin to happen.
100 – 1,000	Yes, your star is starting to shine. Prime time is on your horizon.
1,000 – 5,000	You are making money now.
5,000 +	You are above the crowd and cloud ... welcome to the world of *Best Selling* author ... you rock!

Marketing and People Platform building is never a short term project. It takes a concentrated, targeted plan to triumph in your goals ... and it takes patience and commitment. You don't have to have significant amounts of money to propel it—you can though, lose money and a lot of time going down the wrong track.

Knowing who You and Your Book are; what your strengths and weaknesses; understand what type of media venue you shine best in; and being focused in your strategies guarantees success.

Don't keep the losers and lose your keepers.

As you build your Village … you will find that each expert you use—whether it's a designer, editor, consultant or a printer—has a different talent within a specific function. Some illustrators are hilarious, others more serious; some great with kid themes, others strictly adult. Some printers are amazing with offset but the color isn't so hot. Some editors are perfect for a book on health issues but suck at fiction. Some interior designers excel when art is used but are blah with business books. Some … you get the picture.

And some just don't work—they don't get your book. Period. Your Village will be interactive—they talk amongst themselves and if there is a bad apple, it sours the lot. It's up to you to solve and remove the misfits. If you don't, the ones that you want to work with may just decide it's too much work.

This is your book. You are the author. The final decision maker. If it's not clicking, you need to stop their ticking on your dime. Be loyal to your checkbook, to your book, to your Village and most of all, to yourself.

12

The Money Factor

*Yours Can Be in the Bank, Your Garage
Or Even in the Clouds!*

"Show me the money!"
Cuba Gooding, Jr.
in *Jerry McGuire*

Writing a book isn't a freebie adventure. It's not a "poof," where you have an idea and with a snap of your fingers, it materializes. Nor is the creation and building of your Platforms.

Ideally, it would be wonderful to have all the cash you need to support you and your book sitting in an account that you can withdraw from as the need arrives. Most authors don't work that way—it's more like a piece-meal venture ... dribbling moneys out and sucking it in when the big checks zoom out of the account.

Sure, eBooks cost a lot less ... but, and it's a big BUT ... most of the eBooks today are fairly awful. Why? Start with poor construction of a story or delivery of a problem that the author attempts to find and deliver the solution to. Next up is lack of editing. Follow that with poor design—yes, I know it's an eBook, but it still needs "something" in the interior to hold the reader's eye, and yes, it needs a decent cover.

Print books are a bigger investment—full covers and pages plus the interior design is more extensive.

Where are the seed funds coming from? Your savings? Your equity in the house? A gift? A loan from a relative or friend? The bank (I know, I know—that's a joke!)? The lottery? ... where?

To create and print your book requires a *Spending Plan* aka Budget. What's yours? You can spend $5,000 for cover design, but should you? Most likely, NO ... we know designers who do terrific jobs for $500. Ditto for layout and any graphics. You can do negotiating for editing (i.e. by the project vs. the hour) and even with consultants if you decide to bring them in. Ditto for media and marketing strategies.

When I plan a new book, I budget $10,000 to $15,000 which will include a print run of 3,000 copies. Granted, I don't have to pay for consultants, but I do use editors, layout specialists, cover designers, illustrators and printers. The lower amount would reflect a book that is less than 200 pages and has a minimal use of illustrations.

Whichever avenue you pursue, you need that *Spending Plan*. Whether you fund the entire project with your own hard won dollars, or you seek support/assistance from others, having your plan in writing helps focus yourself, plus it gives your potential "banker" (you or your angel(s)) an idea of overall costs, plus what projected revenues can be.

Have Book Idea, No Money?

The idea of having a project or book that you are passionate about, so passionate about you are willing to do just about anything to get it published, will help you get over the fear, discomfort of asking for investors in your book if need be. Most authors start with their own resources before reaching out to others.

Activity 22
Finding the Money

Start with your own resources. What do you have in: savings, retirement, stocks, stuff, loan options, etc.?

What   **Estimated Value**

_____   _____

_____   _____

_____   _____

_____   _____

_____   _____

_____   _____

_____   _____

_____   _____

Sources to consider include:

Retirement Funds

Usually taboo to tap into … unless you truly believe that your book, with your moxie, your Platforms, planning and marketing skills (and a solid audience) is going to create a return, it's an option. Be careful.

Selling Stuff

Yes, Yes and Yes. If you haven't used it in the last year, let it go. Get ye' to the basement and the garage. Dump for cash. The sooner the better.

Jewelry

Have you got rings, necklaces, bracelets, pins—more stuff—that has gold, silver, diamonds, gems—you name it—and you don't wear them or love them? When the metals started climbing in value, many an old diamond setting found their way to the jeweler. Every major city has resellers. Check prices on Craig's list for a guideline of some sort.

Stocks and other Investments

Your book is a form of investment … that is, if you do it right and have the Passion, Vision and Commitment to support it. Selling your 200 shares of XYZ stock may just be the perfect choice.

Winning the Lottery

Ironically, 25 percent of the American population thinks that they will fund their retirement with winnings from a Lottery. Fat chance. Bypass this one.

Family and Friends

You can go to family and structure an appropriate agreement based on a workable and well laid out budget.

These agreements are an educational process as most family and friends are unfamiliar with the publishing process and its costs. But like so many small businesses, people you know may believe in your ability to make your business/book successful. And, they want to see a well thought out business and publishing plan. Their Catch-22 will be: When will they get their money back?

Do everyone a favor. Consider a solid loan agreement including payment plans and options. Put it in writing.

There's Gold in Your Closets and Garage

Remember cleaning out the clutter ... Now is the time to go through the used CDs and take them and sell them. Old stereo equipment—you won't get much for it, but you will get something—and you will get rid of an item you don't use. Make it a game. If you have some clothes that no longer work for you and are gently worn, take them to a consignment store. You won't get your money tomorrow in most cases but you will get a check in a few months.

There are "vintage stores" that will pay cash on the spot for clothes and items they believe will sell. Don't expect top dollar, but cash is cash if that's what you are looking for. Your fingers are going to need to do the walking on your computer to find them, but it's worth a try.

Furniture can be sold at consignment shops as well. Or, the quickest way is have yourself a garage sale. Learn about staging your sale so it doesn't look like a pile of "stuff." The Goodwill stores have learned that when they set up their displays like regular retailers, their quality of clientele increased as did their sales. I've got several friends who hold annual sales, bringing in thousands of dollars each time—from furniture and other stuff ... some theirs and many cast-offs of others who just didn't want to be bothered.

Peer-to-Peer Lending

Still need more funding and credit cards are maxed? Try peer-to-peer lending. The *Harvard Business Review* reports that this is an increasingly attractive option both for the lender and the borrower.

While this is a relatively unknown option, it is a viable one. Websites such as *www.Prosper.com* match lenders with borrowers and cuts out the middleman.

These websites have created a rapidly growing sector that's slated to climb by 800 percent this year to $5.8 billion in loans, according to research firm, *Celent*. The loans are primarily personal, auto and home-improvement loans, but who says they can't be used to pay for publishing a book? You do need a credit score of 640 or better. Rates generally are 20 to 30 percent better than the banks are offering. Good news; you are usually funded within a couple of days.

The October, 2010 issue of the *Harvard Business Journal* states, "Collaborative consumption is not a niche trend, and it's not a reactionary blip to the recession. It's a socioeconomic groundswell that will transform the way companies think about their value propositions—and the way people fulfill their needs."

Grants

Although not a grant for publishing, the website *www.FundsForWriters.com* lists various foundations which fund writing retreats. Why not write an article or series of articles as a freelancer to get your material out into the marketplace, and get paid to publish in the process? Each article could be a chapter, or at least the genesis of it for your book. With a little planning you can save up your necessary funds to publish your book!

If you have a "current topic," there may be moneys looking for you! One of my clients published his first book that evolved around the future of health care. Within two months of having book in hand, he was offered $10,000 in grant money to seed his next book with a group that discovered his first book. When he told them about his next project, their ears perked up and a discussion started and ended quickly and positively. The group wanted to support his Vision, his Platform. A nice deal for him; no strings attached; and it covered the print cost of his first book. You never know!

Obtaining a grant for anything means that it's tax free—you don't have to report the income, although you may have to report to the grant giver some type of accounting and summary of what you are doing/did. With that said, it's important to say this about grants: obtaining one is not overnight funding. If you choose to tap into this source, check out current books from your local library on grant writing. There are unique phrases and timings to be used to position you better.

Your Book Money May Be in the Clouds ... or the Crowds!

Welcome to the expanding world of cloud funding, also known as crowd funding, crowd source capital or social funding, where authors just might find the right crowd who will support their ideas and book in a combined social networking with project fundraising project.

Well-known authors, like Seth Godin, have used cloud/crowd funding to seed and in some cases, finance their entire book projects (Godin raised $40,000 is less than four hours via *Kickstarter.com*). It always starts with an idea and then the rest is up to you. What are you pitching to your fans, your crowd, your soon-to-be fans and crowd? What are you going to "gift" them if they send $10, $20, $50, $100, $500, $1000 (let's think big!) your way. Do you have DVDs, CDs, another book, a special event that you will host for all ... what?

What's cool about cloud funding is that it's similar to a grant (previous section) than to a loan—as in you don't pay it back. Even the SEC has stepped up to the plate and created a ruling that exempts projects of $20,000 or less and for contributions of $100 or less (if donations exceed $100, make sure you get professional advice). How did the ruling come about? Why, through cloud funding— a successful campaign raised $1,300 to cover the cost of preparing a petition to convince the SEC to "de-regulate" most who are seeking moneys.

Expect most contributions to be under $100—the average project seeks $5,000 with a wide range from $500 to $25,000—so be realistic, set your goals and go for it.

What's interesting is that some will contribute to your cause—the book—just because they like the sound of it or what you are doing.

Once you lay out your presentation on why YOU, why your BOOK and all the other marvelous goodies that come with it on the funding website you partner with (meaning you will pay some type of fundraising fee) … it then goes out to the cyber universe. Savvy authors include a video—stats show that it increases moneys raised by 100 percent plus! YOU, of course, should be letting everyone and their uncle know about the BOOK and project and the link to go to.

Where do you go to learn more (and create your own project)? There's a variety of sites, and surely more to come.

Focusing on the arts in general are: *www.KickStarter.com*, *www.SellaBand.com*, and *www.Pledge.com*. If you have research on your "to do" list or are an investigative journalist, *www.Spot.Us.com* may be perfect for you. The author entrepreneur efforts can also be hatched on *www.IndieGoGo.com* and *www.Invested.In.com* to help a wide range of musicians, writers, filmmakers, game or application developers, designers, inventors, non-profits and charities.

Is there a cost? Yes there is. Expect to fork over up to10 percent of what you raise. Sites like *www.IndieGoGo.com* pay a percentage back if you meet your goal within the time you set. There's one more positive twist for you: if you don't reach your goal, you still keep the money you raise, less the websites' take … and the contributors know that up front!

In publishing, don't rush. It takes time. You need help in the process and it isn't free. You have to pay ... you may have someone that is open to some bartering, but don't expect it.

And don't try to negotiate in the sense that "when your book sells, they can get royalties that will more than offset the cost of their services."

Unless you have a track record of selling books already ... this doesn't cut the mustard.

When you invest in yourself and your book, you become the creator of your future.

Creating a book takes time and money—it's part of the Commitment factor in building your Platforms. Attempting to do it on a shoestring is a challenge from the get-go. Do you have to spend a fortune? No. Can you do one for a few hundred dollars? Yes … but should you? No. It will look like you spent a few hundred dollars—equivalent to a few tanks of gas for a SUV, a weekend at the Fairfield Inn or a few movies and dinner out. Doesn't your Vision, your Passion, your Book, YOU, deserve more?

Don't think of your Book as something that will arrive in a spit and polished format in 30 days. It takes a little time and some negotiating. Save money by getting publishing smart.

- Learn what you need and what you don't need.
- Avoid the growing number of predators that sniff around you and your hard-earned money.
- Use publishing pros that are in the business of books.
- Create a spending plan for your Book.

Embrace the Internet—it will become an essential tool for marketing—and you can do it for free.

13

Your Platforms ... Putting It All Together

An Amazing Journey Begins

"If we advance confidently in the direction of our dreams, and endeavor to live the life we imagine, we will meet with a success unexpected in common hours."

Henry David Thoreau

Does it work? Yes. The numbers will always tell the story. Your book(s) identify you as an expert who has answers and solutions; someone with a gift of storytelling; an inspirer or motivator. Any and all become part of your brand. Your visibility and any speeches you make around the topic of your book add to your expertise and branding. Consulting or coaching around your expertise created from your book and Platforms add to the branding bucket. Sponsorships from corporations can surface and add to your Platforms—making you the go-to person in your field.

Absolutely, a Book and Author Platform create critical components in your author and book persona. Mine created in excess of $4,000,000 over a 20 year span on one theme, one topic. Who knows where and what yours might lead you to!

They take work; they take planning; they take time to create. You will stumble at times, thinking you are in the right direction, discovering that there will be a few mis-directs along the way. I know that I did. Sometimes the dissonance will become so loud that it feels like a total mish-mash of noise; then all of a sudden, it settles into an amazing melody. You've found your rhythm and the music becomes beautiful. The People, the Passion, the Vision and the Time, Energy and Money that goes with the Commitment.

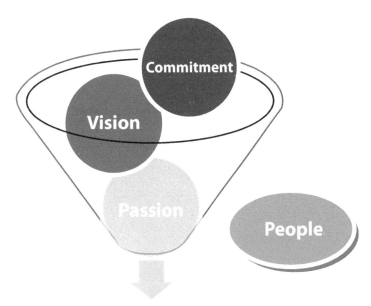

Author and Book Platforms

As I wrote in the Introduction: Your Platforms will always begin with some type of Statement of Fact—why you wrote your book; why you are the author for it; why you are committed to it and its theme/topic; who your readers/crowd/fans/community are and what value you bring. You do it with Confidence, Clarity, Competence and Commitment.

Your Platforms become your core infrastructure. Your Author and Book essence. The word and phrase are no longer just buzz words that are tossed around like a salad ... you get it ... and You and your Book breathe it.

And you now tell other authors traveling the journey, "Don't leave *You* or *Your Book* without your Platforms."

Books don't happen by themselves. Authors aren't created as a solo act. The Village creates both.

As you've built your Platforms, you've created an amazing Village that supported your Vision, Passion and become as Committed to YOU and your Book as you are—one that you will most likely come back to visit again.

The final ingredient in your Book Village are the People—the People who will come.

Make sure you give out the kudos when you get the chance. An Appreciations or Acknowledgement page tells the world who your Village is.

AfterWord

"If a book is not alive in the writer's mind,
it is as dead as year-old horse-shit."

Stephen King

What a journey this thing called publishing is. At this point, your eyes may feel bleary, your body is screaming for another option of activity and your brain … well, your brain might be telling you it's on overload.

Your journey is just beginning. But what a journey you are on. Publishing is a theme park of surprises. At times, you will have your arms in the air, shouting to any and all that you've done it; at others, you experience the darkness of a tunneled ride just waiting for the next thing to spook you.

Having a book, with your name as the author on it, adds a significant notch in the credibility game. It goes beyond just a business card; it becomes part of your guts and soul. There isn't a gathering of people where someone, in fact, many ones, will share that they feel that they have a book in them.

I'm excited that I can be part of this amazing journey that you have chosen. Having published 30 books with my name on the front cover; having the pleasure of working on hundreds of others as I tweaked and helped reword author's words and to express their intent; and having been the midwife to hundreds in the birthing/publishing room, I know what you are going through. Oh, do I know.

Your publishing will create a river of new friends and contacts. As you cross the bridge, you will meet people, gather fans that you never imagined would hang on to each word and idea you created and have a fabulous time. Send me a postcard, a tweet (@MyBookShepherd), post a comment on my Facebook page (Dr Judith Briles or The Book Shepherd) or an email (Judith@Briles.com) along your way.

Your Platforms will become the infrastructure of what you and your book are about. With them, you and your book are on solid ground—just where you want to be.

The Publishing Siren has beckoned. Welcome to my world—Author YOU.

Judith

Appreciations

No book is a solo act. The authors are always up front … we get to take the bows. Yet, it's all the players behind the scenes that really bring our words to you. The creation of Author YOU was no small task.

I tip my writing pen to John Maling who edits quickly; to Georgann Hall who adds her eagle eye in the final pass and my clients and publishing colleagues who said, "I wish I had had this when I first started writing."

True to my muse, I finished this book with the trappings of the Royal Caribbean Cruise Line—a little sun in the Caribbean, sprinkled with two days of snorkeling and swimming, and I was good for 10 days of intense writing and polishing. If there's some sea salt on these pages, you know where it came from!

Doug Gilbert and Tim Clark seeded my visual think tank over lunch when Tim wanted my input for the marketing of his new book, *Business Model You* … I immediately saw that we were so in synch. *Author YOU* had already been written and the first draft layout done. After meeting Tim, I saw a new vision for displaying the *Author YOU* roadmap, the one that you are holding that was designed by Nick Zelinger.

Ahhh … thanks to the amazing Nick who has always added to the book pie with his interiors and cover designs—and he didn't throw a pie at me when I suggested (as in, "Hey Nick, what do you think about changing the book you've already designed—let's switch and do a landscape format—more room to do all the Activities in and let's add a bunch more visuals … oh, and let's add color everywhere, and …"

Thanks to Don Sidle who added the flair of his whimsical illustrations throughout and was always open with a twist and a tweak here and there.

Thanks to my many clients who have always sparked my imagination, often with the question, "Can I …."
and my response has always been, "Why not …"

And of course, thanks to the members of the Author U community who constantly ask questions; encourage
other authors on their journey and who make the ride so much more fun.

Who is Judith Briles?

Judith Briles is the founder and co-founder of several companies and organizations including Mile High Press, Ltd., a small press that has published 13 titles (*www.MileHighPress.com*), The Book Shepherd (*www.TheBookShepherd.com*), a company that works with authors to create, strategize, develop and publish their books; and Author U (*www.AuthorU.org*), a membership association dedicated to the serious author who wants to create quality books and achieve financial success. Her radio show, *Your Guide to Book Publishing with Dr. Judith Briles*, can be heard on the *RockStartRadioNetwork.com*.

She has been teaching workshops on publishing since 1984, and working with authors who are in the beginning stages of their books to implement an over-all plan to achieve book success. Judith Briles is known as The Book Shepherd. She knows publishing through the wearing of multiple hats: award-winning publisher (multiple first place awards for business, how to and publishing technology printing, lay-out and cover design), author (*Chicago Tribune's* Business Book of the Year, Colorado Book of the Year) and book advisor. The books of her clients routinely win awards in multiple publishing and author contests.

Judith is an award-winning author of 30 books, to date, including: *Show Me About Book Publishing* (co-written with John Kremer and Rick Frishman), *Stabotage!™ How to Deal with Pit Bulls, Skunks, Snakes, Scorpions & Slugs in the Health Care Workplace, Zapping Conflict in the Health Care Workplace, The Confidence Factor: Cosmic Gooses Lay Golden Eggs, Stop Stabbing Yourself in the Back, Woman to Woman: From Sabotage to Support, Woman to Woman 2000: Becoming Sabotage Savvy in the New Millennium,*

Money Smarts for Turbulent Times, Smart Money Moves for Kids and *10 Smart Money Moves for Women.*
Author YOU: Creating and Building Your Author and Book Platforms is her 30th book. Her first book,
The Woman's Guide to Financial Savvy was published in 1981 by St. Martin's Press. To date, her books have
been translated in 16 foreign countries.

Her work has been featured in the *Wall Street Journal, Newsweek, Time, People, USA Today, Self,
The New York Times* and *People* magazine. She has been a frequent guest on national television and
radio and has appeared on over 1,000 programs, including CNN, *Oprah* and *Good Morning America.*
Judith writes regularly for a variety of publications.

Judith is a past president of The Colorado Author's League, and is a past director of the National
Speaker's Association; Gilda's Club-Denver; The WISH List; the Women's Bank and the Colorado Women's
Leadership Coalition and serves on several private corporation boards. Currently, she is Chief Visionary Officer of Author U and CEO of The Book Shepherd.

Colorado Biz magazine has named one of her companies as a Top 100 in Colorado. She is honored to
be named the Woman of Distinction by the Girl Scouts of America.

www.JudithBrilesUnplugged.com
www.TheBookShepherd.com

Working with Judith

Judith Speaks ... Would You Like to Listen? She would be delighted to participate in your publishing conference or to speak to your group. Her expertise is all things authoring and publishing—creating the book, getting it in print and strategizing its launch and marketing plan. If you want a highly interactive, informative and fun presentation or workshop, call her.

Her dynamic presentations include:

Author YOU ... Creating and Building Your Book and Author Platforms

The Dollars, Cents & Sense of Publishing

Is There a Book in You?

Creating Your Book Launch

It Takes a Village to Create a Book

Show Me About Book Publishing

Beware of Pit Bulls, Snakes and Publishing Predators

Do you need Book Shepherding or Coaching? Judith is The Book Shepherd and works with a variety of authors both domestically and internationally. Some books are from scratch, some are in process and some are completed, ready for the first edit others are already written.

To determine if your book is one that would work with her expertise and involvement or to ask about availability for speaking at your conference or creating a workshop for your group, call or email:

Dr. Judith Briles
303-885-2207
Judith@Briles.com
Judith@TheBookShepherd.com
www.TheBookShepherd.com
www.AuthorU.org
www.Briles.com
www.JudithBrilesUnplugged.com

Facebook: JudithBriles, TheBookShepherd, AuthorU (do a "like")
Twitter: @MyBookShepherd, @AuthorU (follow)
LinkedIn: Judith Briles (connect), Author U (join group)
Pinterest: Judith Briles (follow)
Blog: www.TheBookShepherd.com (follow)

Next in the
Author YOU series

In *Author YOU—Creating a Successful Book Launch to Generate Massive Book Sales*, you will get templates, a step-by-step strategy on how create a successful book launch incorporating both social media and morphed marketing strategies and much more.

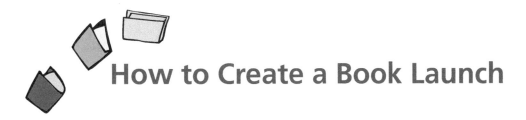

How to Create a Book Launch

"He is able who thinks he is able."
Buddha

The work that you put into the creation of your Author and Book Platforms will lead to your Book Launch. And book sales. Some launches are done as soon as the book is available—be it print, "e" or audio format. Others postpone their launch dates. Think of your Book Launch as a celebration ... the public birthday of your Book.

A Book Launch does not have to be restricted to a new book. There's no reason why you can't launch a book that has been around the block a few times. Some authors never put a thought into creating a special event to kick-start their book until it has been out for a while.

Book Launch: A marketing strategy created by an author and/or his team to create buzz and sales for his book. Usually done through the Internet with several partners who have networks, encouraging each of them within it to buy the book on a specific day through a specific source. Amazon, Barnes & Noble and the Author's Home page are the most common points of purchase. The Launch can range from a day to several days.

You can coordinate all the details yourself or you can hire someone to do it for you. The key components of a successful Book Launch include:

- A specific website that is exclusively about your Book Launch;

- Joint venture partners who will tell their members within their networks and recommend your Book;

- Gifts and bonuses to give to those who purchase your Book;

- Blogs that will either review your book or ask you do to a guest blog on the day of your Launch;

- A coordinated campaign that reaches out to multiple social media channels including Facebook, Google+, Twitter, LinkedIn, YouTube and Pinterest;

- Books to fill the demand;

- A clear calendar the day before, the day of and the next several days to coordinate your follow-up campaign;

- You to be rested—you will work your butt off staying on top of it;

- Intergrating social media to soar your Book launch; and

- What's new in the ever-changing "As the Amazon Bestseller World Turns."

Authors and Publishing Pros Are Talking … and Talking!

Judith Briles knows publishing. She cuts through the myriad of details and snafus that authors face, saving them thousands of dollars in the publishing process.

Judith has authored and published more than 20 books, won multiple awards and has converted her expertise into savvy, doable strategies for authors who want to create, achieve and be financially successful.

Dan Poynter
The Self-Publishing Manual

Judith Briles is a dynamo who's helped a number of hopeful authors break into the publishing industry. It's simply amazing to watch her work. It was a great day when I discovered her.

Ward Lucas
Emmy® Award winner and author of *Neighbors at War!*

Judith Briles is one of the most strategically creative, professional and competent people I have met in my 20+ years in book publishing.

Brian Jud
How to Make Real Money Selling Books

Publishing consultants should know publishing inside and out. Few do. Judith Briles does. She has worn many hats—she's published with major New York houses, then broke away and created her own imprint; has successfully published over 20 books and sold in excess of 1,000,000 copies; understands niche publishing and marketing; has created publicity campaigns for her own work.

She has guided and coached many others from creation to completion of their work; she has created and chaired several publishing conferences; and she has successfully turned several publishing disasters into successful outcomes for their authors.

Judith Briles is The Book Shepherd.

Rick Frishman
Publisher, Morgan James Publishing
Founder, Author 101 University

Judith Briles' *Author YOU: Creating and Building your Author and Book Platforms* should be required reading for all authors who want to succeed in the new world of publishing. Her wise counsel combined with reader participating through Questions and Activities will guide you to real success in building your author platform. Highly recommended.

Joel Friedlander
Marin Bookworks, author of *A Self-Publisher's Companion*
www.TheBookDesigner.com

I can't think of another person who has the breadth of experience that Judith Briles does, when it comes to books, publishing, writing—and the art and business that swirls around all of these concepts.

Judith knows this biz from every angle: As a writer, editor, publisher, speaker, consultant and entrepreneur. She's also fabulously creative and wonderfully honest. She's a breath of fresh air in an industry full of poseurs.

Greg Godek
1001 Ways to be Romantic

I will be grateful, always, to Judith Briles for mentoring me—the only mentor I have ever had! She has had such a positive impact on my life. I try—every single day—to pass that gift on ...

Marilyn Van Derbur
Miss America by Day

Judith Briles should be used by anyone in the process of writing or publishing a book. Judith not only saved my book, she helped me create a best-seller! Her energy, wisdom, support, insights, humor and willingness to uphold her commitment were inspirational. As a first time author, my learning curve was quite steep. Judith supported me every step of the process. She went beyond her original job description, always making sure all my needs were met.

Her integrity was exemplary. Not only did we collaborate and complete my book, she then led me through the publishing aspects and now the marketing. I am truly grateful for Judith and her gifts, insights and knowledge. My book would not have happened without her! I highly recommend.

Dr. Lynn Hellerstein
See It. Say It. Do It!

Judith helped us out of what could have been a terrible bind and pointed us squarely in the right direction. She knows oodles and oodles of ins, outs, nuances plus she has the personal connections to do ANYTHING with books, publishing, writing, plus, plus, plus. Her integrity in the community is A+. Our only regret is we wished we had reached out to her earlier. We would have saved a lot of time, heartache and money if we had. She continues to play an important part in our planning and actions.

Mike O'Neil and Lori Ruff
Rock the World with Your Online Presence

Judith Briles works dynamically and effectively to empower others in their quest for success in authoring and publishing. A highly successful author, speaker and publisher herself, she is unstoppable on behalf of her clients and colleagues. Where no apparent solution exists, she invents one. Judith doesn't do the work for you—she shows you how to do it and create the breakthrough you've been looking for.

Mara Purl
Haven Books, BelleKeep Books

I am just very grateful that I met you, and for your incredible support, and your true shepherd wisdom that you contributed to me on this journey of publishing *A New Language for Life, Happy No Matter What!*

Francesca and I feel blessed by the friendship we have developed. We adore your straightforwardness, your ability to call things by its name, and the grace with which at times you responded to my unreasonable requests!

Dr. Louis Koster
A New Language for Life, Happy No Matter What!

You just finished a masterpiece, just put your creative passion into it, and now don't know what to do about it? Call for the assistance of Judith Briles, The Book Shepherd. Judith has the knowledge at her fingertips from taking your idea and putting it into words to finding the right editors and the right printers. Need advice on how to market your book? She has a myriad of ideas and knowledge of the ways to do it. Judith is an extraordinary woman who will be YOUR personal book shepherd.

She has been there for us through good and bad, happiness and frustration. We don't know what we would do without her calmness—when we sometimes feel max-frustration.

Georgann and Jim Hall
Parachuting for Gold in Old Mexico

After eight months without success, my book project needed rescuing when I recognized that the best written book without quality marketing will only be read by my family, friends, and perhaps my teddy bear. I soon learned that book publishing is more than writing an outstanding book and putting a nice cover on it. Judith and Author U. (which she founded) guided me through the intricacies of book publishing. Her referral network (to create the book cover, layout etc.) was outstanding. She also helped me select which award competitions were appropriate.

To date, my book has won three book awards for overall book quality in 2012 including the National Indie Excellence Award in the Relationships category, the Sponsors Award (Given to the top 8 of NIEA in any category with benefits worth $1,300), and the Global eBook Awards for Parenting/Family Nonfiction. Thank you Judith for a job well done!

Roger Frame, Ph.D.
Don't Carve the Turkey with a Chainsaw: Resolving Family Conflict

I can't imagine trying to make my way through the writing, editing and publishing process of a book without Judith's "shepherding." I have watched Judith customize her approach to meet the needs of the individual author. That's priceless! I love a no-nonsense, get-it-done approach and Judith was that for me. Not only was Judith a guide in getting my book to reality, she taught me an immeasurable amount about the process. I think I will do this again—but not without Judith!

Debbie Wilde, author of *The Sustainable Nonprofit*

A shepherd is defined as one who "protects, guides, and watches over." That's exactly what Judith Briles brings to your book and/or speaking project. She won't write your book for you, but she protects you from making senseless mistakes, she guides you through the meticulous process, and she watches over your journey from beginning to end. Working with Judith is one of the best investments I've made in my business.

Dom Testa, Radio Talk Show Host
The Galahad series
The Big Brain Club

Judith Briles is my BOOK SHEPHERD and has been for many years. She guided me through my first book, *The PeaceFinder—Riley McFee's Quest for World Peace.* She is now helping me publish my husband's autobiography as well as a book I have written on parenting plans for divorced parents. It would be very difficult to get through the publishing maze without her. She knows the business, has amazing vision, and is remarkably creative. She can spot errors in an instant, which saves money!

I have enjoyed getting to know Judith and count her as a friend as well as a mentor. Working with her has been my good fortune.

Joan McWilliams
The Peace Finder
Parenting Plans That Work

Judith Briles is a joy to work with. She has a firm foundation for assisting and directing individuals on their own path. One of the things I like most of Judith is that she supported me in keeping to my own path, my own voice, rather than one that has worked for others. Authenticity is a key ingredient to success and Judith connected my intentions to my authenticity...creating incredible results.

Barbara Joye Radcliffe
The Creating Formula

If you need a firm, yet compassionate, kick in the bum to get your writing project completed and out the door, Judith Briles is not only the clear choice—but the greatest value. Don't spend a lot of money on a bunch of different consultants on writing and publishing; work with Judith first to help you create the best team for your writing project and increase your efficiency. Her salons with other authors cannot be beat, with one-on-one follow-up to keep you on track.

Susan E. Mead, M.H.
Take Back Your Body

Judith is a tireless advocate for authors and independent publishing; the knowledge and skills that she contributes to each project allow authors to produce top quality work and results that exceed expectations. She has a gift for knowing how best to spotlight an author's strengths, and her vast network of connections and resources ensure that authors are working with top notch professionals in all aspects of the publishing process. Judith also focuses on evaluating challenges authors are experiencing and developing solutions to keep the momentum and energy going in the right direction. Whether you are a new or veteran author, her creativity and expertise will take you to the next level in producing a superior book.

Kelly Johnson
The Virtuous Assistant to Authors
at Cornerstone Virtue Assistance

Judith Briles is an incredible book advisor. She is the most knowledgeable person I have met in the book business. Her workshops are informative, well-organized and fun and give budding authors inspiration as well as encouragement. Judith sets high standards for herself and also her clients—she is never afraid to tell it like it is. She encourages her clients to be their personal best. Judith's vast knowledge and experience in both publishing and marketing make her an invaluable resource. She takes a personal interest in the authors she works with; and despite a very busy work schedule, she is only a telephone call away when problems arise and need immediate solutions. I would highly recommend Judith Briles.

Carol Ann Kates
Secret Recipes from the Corner Market

Thank you Judith Briles, for all the guidance through the minefields of being an author. You are truly the "Book Shepherd."

Doug Krug
The Missing Piece in Leadership

To be honest, I was a bit overwhelmed and scared with the idea of writing a book. I just knew I had to tell my story to help raise awareness and help others on their journey. I was referred to The Book Shepherd by a dear friend. After meeting with Judith, I felt a sense of comfort. She helped guide me through the entire process, and we met my goal to have my book in my possession in just eight months. I want to say thank you Judith, for helping me on this journey to make this dream of mine become a reality.

Luci Berardi
Chasing Rainbows

Judith made me feel welcome, showed real enthusiasm for my project and, in the face of doubt and anxiety, boosted my confidence. She is a well-connected general contractor, coordinating a cadre of seasoned subcontractors. In addition, her expertise and coaching for the book promotion process really shines. She anticipated real world expenses and production potholes I would never have considered. Judith knew how to put together a budget for all the steps of my project. I liked the way she trimmed the fluff out of a production contract and book promotion campaign. Her reasonable project fees were more than offset by the savings gained from what I would have spent while trying to go it all alone.

She showed me how to improve my book—its cover copy, preface, introduction, authors' bio and more—leveling with me about where to make rewrites and offered ideas about how to accomplish them. When it came to book promotion and distribution, she frequently reminded me of ways to promote my book early, providing many clues about how to do it. Without her urging, I would be much further behind in my book promotion campaign. This meant she pushed me out of my comfort zone and inspired me to learn new ways of connecting with readers, and how to present my messages in more reader friendly styles.

I recommend Judith to anyone who wants to offer readers more than a book—instead, a reading adventure—whether electronic, paper or audio. She knows the business. I am looking forward to working with her as we move into the doubly intense phase of promoting and publicizing.

Gene Morton
Leaders First: Six Bold Steps to Sustain Breakthroughs in Construction

Judith Briles, The Book Shepherd, Recommends ...

If you are an Author who wants to be Seriously Successful, Judith recommends that you join Author U, an organization that is dedicated to your success. It does it by delivering *The Resource* ezine, weekly blogs, extensive Twitter, Facebook, LinkedIn, Pinterest presence and postings, monthly programs, webinars, teleseminars, a weekly radio show—*Your Guide to Book Publishing*, semi-annual BookCamps and the annual Author U Extravaganza held the first weekend in May.

Join at www.AuthorU.org

"Author U is the premier authoring resource in the country creating community, education, guidance, vision and success for the serious author."

Judith Briles, The Book Shepherd, Recommends …

Experience two full days of Judith every fall—the first Friday and Saturday of September … no guest speakers, no pitches, just **Judith Briles Unplugged** delivering an amazing depth of publishing, authoring and marketing information that she has derived from her 30 plus years in the publishing field and as The Book Shepherd.

- If you are just starting down the authoring and publishing path, you will come away with a personalized strategy to create and develop your book.

- If your book is ready to birth, you will come away with amazing steps and ahas on how to soar its official launch and develop your next steps.

- If your book is currently available, no matter how old, your current marketing concepts and strategies will be turned upside down.

Judith Briles Unplugged is not just another publishing conference where you sit in your seat and take notes—expect extraordinary high interaction, plenty of "to-do" Activities—you will not only listen and hear The Book Shepherd, you will immediately implement what she says. Judith believes in feeding your brain and your belly. It is your next, next step to authoring and book success. Be there. Register below and use the code *unplugged*—save $50.

www.JudithBrilesUnplugged.com

Notes

Notes

Notes

Notes